Arguments for Socialism

Series editor: John Harrison

Arguments for Socialism is a series of popular and provocative books which deal with the economic and political crisis in Britain today. The series argues the need for a radical rethinking of major political questions and contributes to the debates on strategy for the left.

'One of the main reasons why the Tories swept to power in 1979 was that the Labour movement had over the years almost ceased to argue for socialism. This series, *Arguments for Socialism*, can play a significant part in re-establishing the necessity for a socialism that is democratic, libertarian and humane.' *Tony Benn*

Other **Arguments for Socialism**

The Cuts Machine

The Politics of Public Expenditure

David Hall

Pluto **AP** Press

First published in 1983 by Pluto Press Limited,
The Works, 105a Torriano Avenue,
London NW5 2RX

British Library Cataloguing in Publication Data
Hall, David   The cuts machine.—(Arguments for socialism)
1. Great Britain—Appropriations and expenditures—History—20th century
2. Great Britain—Politics and government—1964–
I. Title   II. Series
338.5'4   HB3716
ISBN 0-86104-504-1

Cover designed by Clive Challis A Gr R
Cover photograph: Michael Abrahams, Network
Computerset by Promenade Graphics Limited
Block 23a Lansdown Industrial Estate, Cheltenham GL51 8PL
Printed and bound in Great Britain
by Richard Clay (The Chaucer Press) Limited, Bungay, Suffolk

Contents

Preface

This book is about the politics of public services and public spending. While public services matter to people and socialism, public spending is a problem for bankers and capitalism. The following chapters aim to show how public services suffer at the hands of those who are concerned with the problem of public spending.

The 'cuts machine' described here is not the cause of the cuts, just the way they get made. The economic and political forces and conflicts which do cause the cuts are illustrated, however, by the workings of the machine. The administrative and economic technicalities which are often taken for granted in discussions of public services are themselves politically loaded.

Public services matter because they put need before profit, caring before selling, people before prestige. Or rather, they should. Political attacks on services strangle these values. Political fights for services advance them. Recognising the machine and disarming it are parts of this fight.

Acknowledgements

This book arises out of work done in the research department of the Society of Civil and Public Servants to assist campaigns against cuts from 1976 onwards. Much of that work was done with research officers of other public service unions, especially Alan Churchard of the Civil and Public Services Association.

Parts of Chapter 5 are based on a joint union pamphlet *Behind Closed Doors*, published in 1979 by the National Steering Committee Against the Cuts. Parts of Chapter 6 originate from a paper published by the Trade Union Research Unit in 1982. Sections of Chapter 7 are based on material which was previously used for two articles in the *New Statesman* in 1981.

Thanks are due to all those workers in the public services on whose knowledge and experience this book draws freely. Thanks too to a number of people for help, encouragement, comments on drafts, typing and general support: Campbell Christie, Geoff Hall, Ethne Hall, Helen Issler, Ian Linn, Steve Lord, Judy Mallaber, Richard Norton-Taylor, Peta Sissons, Sally Watson, Dexter Whitfield. Thanks also to John Harrison for being a patient, stimulating and constructive editor. The defects of the book remain the author's responsibility.

Abbreviations

AES	Alternative Economic Strategy
AUEW	Amalgamated Union of Engineering Workers
CBI	Confederation of British Industry
CSE	Conference of Socialist Economists
DES	Department of Education and Science
DHSS	Department of Health and Social Security
FIS	Financial Information System
GLC	Greater London Council
GMWU	General and Municipal Workers' Union
GNP	Gross National Product
IMF	International Monetary Fund
NALGO	National and Local Government Officers Association
PAC	Public Accounts Committee
PESC	Public Expenditure Survey Committee
PSBR	Public Sector Borrowing Requirement
RAWP	Resource Allocation Working Party
RPI	Retail Price Index
RSG	Rate Support Grant
TGWU	Transport and General Workers' Union
TUC	Trades Union Congress
UGC	University Grants Commission
VFM	'Value-for-money' auditing

1.

The Story of the Cuts

This book is the story, among other things, of why big business cannot afford for children to have school meals. It is also the story of how the City of London stopped council houses being built, of health workers being kept on low pay to subsidise multinationals' profits, of claimants helping build up the Bank of England's reserves, and why private enterprise wants to clean government offices.

Cuts made by successive governments since 1974 have produced these results. In the process, full use has been made of a whole set of administrative systems, accounting conventions and financial practices, which together make up a powerful machine geared precisely to cutting back public services.

The machine does not have a life of its own. From time to time it may be left idling in neutral. Under pressure, it may even be forced into reverse for brief periods. But since the mid-70s it has been driven steadily forwards, grinding public services as it goes. This chapter looks at the cuts it has been used to make, and how they developed. Later chapters examine the components of the machine.

Crisis

The crisis which sparked off the cuts started in the early 1970s, and was not confined to Britain. Inflation soared to record levels, real profitability fell, and production and investment fell in sympathy. Detailed analyses of this crisis have been given elsewhere and will not be repeated here.

In addition, there had been since 1970 increasing industrial relations problems in the public sector. Postal workers, miners, electricians, council workers, teachers, health workers and civil servants had all taken industrial action in pay disputes. The health service, local government and the civil service had all been reorganised, partly to strengthen managerial controls over workers. In February 1974 a government fell as a direct result of a miners' strike. These disputes were followed by exceptionally large pay increases to teachers, nurses and others in 1974.

Economists, politicians and the media all began to focus on public spending as the key to the crisis. It was said to be out of control, inflationary, wasteful and consuming vital resources that could be used more productively and profitably.

The 1970s was not the first time that a cutback in public spending had been seen as a solution to an economic crisis. In 1931 a similar response had been adopted by a Labour Government which cut benefits as a way of tackling economic problems. Indeed, public expenditure has almost by definition been regarded as an economic problem in itself, from eighteenth-century anxieties over the national debt, to the 1960s when a new control system was introduced which gave the Treasury more power to stop spending.

This presumption against public spending, which is considered in more detail in the next chapter, has always been politically opposed to the socialist vision of public services as collective provision for social needs. From 1974 onwards this conflict became a central political battle.

A massive wave of propaganda was unleashed to support the attacks on public services. The media dusted down and replayed the traditional vilifications of public employees as idle, bloated parasites living off the backs of the rest of us. A group of economists popularised the view that poor British industrial performance was due to the over-inflated burden of the unproductive public services, and this found an echo in sections of the Labour Party and the TUC who believed it was necessary to reverse the 'de-industrialisation' of Britain whereby ever fewer workers were employed in manufacturing. The government argued that public spending had to give way to the needs of productive industry. Most of this material was within the main Keynesian tradition of economic planning, which could still represent the cuts as an exercise in planned redistribution of resources from over-provisioned sectors to the economic frontline: despite the clear evidence that the 'frontline' – manufacturing companies – neither needed nor intended to take on extra people or even investment.

The major new contribution came from the doctrine of monetarism. This won widespread support for its central theme that both inflation and poor industrial performance were due to excessive borrowing by governments, and that the aim of maintaining employment by expanding public spending was doomed to make things worse – a 'natural' level of unemployment was unavoidable. The public sector borrowing requirement (PSBR) shot to prominence as the root of all evil, and anything that reduced the PSBR became a good thing.

Labour's cuts for business

The Labour government's first major response to the crisis came in the November 1974 mini-budget, which aimed to boost company profits. Companies received tax relief on the increase in the value of their stocks, which had risen sharply with inflation. This relief was backdated, and amounted at the time to a handout of over £2,500 million – over 3½ per cent of total National Income. The following month, price controls were relaxed to boost profitability further, at the cost of increasing retail prices by 1½ per cent.

These measures made clear that profitability was – and was to remain – the central concern of economic policy. The inevitable increase in government borrowing that arose – not only from the tax relief but from the effects of inflation and recession – put further pressure on the government to cut public spending.

It responded in the April 1975 budget. This increased indirect taxation on consumer spending, and cut public spending by £1 billion. It also contained the first announcement that public spending could be subject to cash limits on the amount of money available, so that if prices and wages rose above a certain level, services and jobs would have to be cut. While companies were being protected against inflation, services were made to suffer from it.

The rest of 1975 saw the consolidation of these policies, against a background of pressures from the financial markets. The first of a series of runs on the pound led to the announcement in July of an incomes policy, agreed to by the TUC, which suspended comparability pay machinery in the civil service and which was to be enforced in the public sector through the setting of the cash limits. Major cuts in public spending were prepared, and local councils were told that 'the party's over', they were advised to plan for no increases in 1976–77.

The key features of the systematic attacks on public services had all emerged by the end of 1975. Profitability was given pride of place over social needs. Taxation policy was used to shift the burden away from capital and onto workers and consumers. Government policies were adjusted in deference to the 'confidence' of the financial markets. New controls were imposed on public spending while controls on companies were relaxed. Attacks were made on public sector workers' pay and conditions. The cuts machine had been set in motion – under a Labour government, and with TUC acquiescence.

The major cuts packages were all announced during 1976, the 'year of the cuts'. The first White Paper in February, contained cuts totalling £4,600 million, at 1976 values, for 1977–78 and 1978–79. In July, a new package cut a further £1,000 million from the plans for 1977–78. December brought the third package, cutting a further £1,000 million from 1977–78 and £1,500 million from 1978–79. In all, spending for 1977–78 was cut by £3,600 million, and for 1978–79 by £4,500 million. Included in these cuts were specific targets for eliminating jobs in local councils and the civil service.

The implementation of the new cash limits system also came in 1976. This set maximum totals of cash which could be spent on each service, and so services were cut if prices rose more than allowed for – and administrators feared to spend even the full amount. Further administrative curbs were imposed, including using the contingency reserve – previously just a sum used to allow for any unforeseen needs – as a Treasury ceiling on any political decisions to improve services. The control system was massively strengthened by this development: public services were firmly subordinated to the confidence of financiers. The priority for the public services was now the reduction of the public sector borrowing requirement (PSBR).

The cuts had the effect intended. By 1978–79, the last year of the Labour government, non-defence spending was 8½ per cent lower than in 1975–76 – excluding social security benefits, which had risen by 18½ per cent because of unemployment. Civil service jobs had fallen by fifteen thousand, and council jobs returned only briefly to the 1975–76 level. Food subsidies were reduced, rents and charges were increased, and counter-inflation policy simply meant, as one cabinet minister put it, 'in current language, pay'. The price code was relaxed further to the point of being meaningless, further tax concessions were given to industry, but indirect taxes and National Insurance contributions were increased. Tables 1 and 2 show how spending was cut, and how cash limits contributed to this (see pp. 107–8).

The public spending White Paper of February 1976, and its successor in January 1977, were both rejected by parliament and followed by motions of no confidence. They were nevertheless implemented in full. Cash limits were never given parliamentary sanction until 1979, but still operated as the overriding control mechanism. The role of social policy in planning public spending became negligible, and departmental officials stated that programmes ceased to be drawn up on the basis of the needs of the services after 1975. By 1978 the Labour government had already begun the battle, later completed by the Tories, to force Southwark Area Health Authority to treat observance of its cash limit as a higher priority than maintaining its local health service.

Women were forced back into (unpaid) domestic service. Cuts in public spending hit a key area of female employment. Lost services had to be made up by the traditional woman's role as domestic provider. The most explicit expression of withdrawal of state from family responsibility was when the cabinet and the TUC expressed an embarrassingly publicised reluctance to introduce child benefit to replace tax allowances – because it meant transferring money 'from the wallet to the handbag'. The male industrial worker at the head of his family remained the focus of policy. The arguments for saving jobs and state benefits by supporting employment levels were used to justify public spending to rescue Chrysler UK from collapse in 1975; the same arguments failed to halt the destruction of public service jobs.

Financiers who dominated the money markets were un-equivocal in their demands for ever tougher policies. They still refused to grant 'confidence' to the government, despite the incomes policy established in 1975. The major cuts package of January 1976, and the introduction of cash limits. There were further runs on the pound in 1976, which led the government to seek loans first from other governments and then from the International Monetary Fund (IMF). These loans were *not* to finance public spending, as was frequently implied by the media, but to boost reserves to strengthen the pound. Amidst widespread publicity, an IMF team visited London in November 1976 to lay down their conditions for the loan. These included not merely further cuts, but a government commit-ment to keep within announced targets for the PSBR and the money supply – the central requirements of monetarist policy.

It was not a case of an unwilling government adopting IMF policies against its better judgement. That judgement had already been made a year earlier, in deciding that the cuts required by the finance markets were to take precedence over any political commitments. Cuts totalling £5,600 million were announced in 1976 before the IMF team arrived, and a public commitment had been made to reduce the PSBR. Indeed, the Treasury forecast of the PSBR was used as the prime justifica-tion for the cuts in July 1976 as well as for the IMF cuts in December, although it was widely – and correctly, as it turned out – criticised as being unrealistically exaggerated. The ex-change rate was also deliberately depressed by the government to help generate conditions favourable to its chosen policies.

Nor were the policies changed when the need for IMF support for sterling was over. At the end of 1977, when the loans had been repaid, Healey nevertheless announced that he would continue to adhere to the policy guidelines laid down by the IMF. During that year, a considerable shortfall in public spending, and a flow of loans from the newly confident markets, were used to build up the reserves. But the financiers continued to keep the government dancing to their tune by a naked exercise of bargaining power – investment strikes took place if the City regarded a government bond as not offering a generous enough return, and in February 1979 a new issue, at unbelievably favourable rates of return, had dealers physically fighting on the steps of the Bank of England for such easy pickings.

The Tory takeover

By the time the Thatcher government took power some key policy objectives had already been established by its predecessor. Some shared objectives were: the restoration of industrial profitability; the necessity of controlling public spending in order to observe declared targets for the PSBR and the money supply; the principle that cash curbs overrode any policy objectives for the public services; the principle that public service jobs were an economic burden, and that public service pay was an engine of inflation; and the acceptance that 'economic recovery' meant the abandonment of full employment as a policy objective.

The Tories took over these objectives and added new refinements of their own. The continuity was highlighted in the first few months of the new government, when Tory ministers were able to quote their Labour predecessors, in defence of Tory policies against Labour opposition in parliament.

The new attacks on the public services began within weeks of the new government taking office, with the announcement of major cuts in spending plans. Labour's plans for 1980–81 were cut by 4 per cent, and for 1982–83 by 8 per cent. Cash limits were deliberately set to impose a further cut of 3 per cent in 1979–80, and declarations were made that public service jobs would be reduced still further. The level of government support to councils was cut by reducing the amount of council spending covered by the government's annual grant (the Rate Support Grant). And, after allowing the pay settlements of the 1979 disputes to go through, a rigid incomes policy was again imposed on the public services through cash limits.

The attack was selective. Spending on defence and on law and order was actually increased, and the previous government's special treatment of police and armed forces pay was continued. The defence budget was given the unique privilege of going beyond its cash limit, but the public services generally continued to be squeezed.

There were innovations from the Tories, too. Social security benefits, which had remained largely immune from Labour's cuts, came under systematic attack, with contributory benefits like unemployment and sickness benefits being particularly harshly reduced in value. Council rents were forced up and council house building drastically cut at the same time as council house sales became mandatory. Industrial support through grants and the National Enterprise Board, and employment and training support through the Manpower Services Commission, were also hit, in line with the new policy of opposition to state intervention in business affairs. Nationalised industries were subjected not only to further requirements to raise prices, and more stringent limits on their ability to borrow, but also to legislation eroding their monopolies of service and to sales of profitable sections – the programme of privatisation.

Other forms of privatisation were also introduced. Private health and private education were explicitly encouraged to develop as alternatives to public services. This was accompanied by more intense erosion of political requirements of public services, which included a wave of legislation in 1980 weakening the statutory obligation on public authorities to provide services such as nursery education, psycho-geriatric care, or to build to certain housing standards. As these controls – which supported services – were reduced, new controls were imposed on the finance available to councils.

More damaging erosion of political support for public services came from new controls over local authorities, introduced not only through legislation but also through an upsurge of activity by district auditors and judges. In 1981 Lothian council in Scotland was forced to make cuts by order of the Secretary of State. The GLC in England discovered that its ability to pursue the cheap fares policies on which it had been elected was severely curtailed by a House of Lords' judgement.

By contrast, the controls over companies were further eroded. The final remains of price controls were scrapped, controls on taking money out of the country were lifted, and attempts were made to set up 'enterprise zones' where planning constraints do not apply. The whole structure of policy was designed to give maximum freedom to profitable activity while curbing public services.

Public employees also faced intensified attacks on their jobs and conditions. In local councils, the NHS and central government alike, auditors were used by the government – with every encouragement from MPs – to guide employers as to how best to get rid of 'wasteful' staff. Sir Derek Rayner was brought in from Marks and Spencer to review civil service activities and recommend ways of cutting jobs. Similar encouragement was given to those involved in business to look at ways of sorting out council staffing. And yet another form of privatisation was introduced, this time a switch from directly employed labour to contract labour from the private sector. This was done by requiring local authorities to tender out more building work, with stringent financial requirements imposed for the continuation of direct labour organisations. The civil service was told to use private cleaners whenever – as is usually the case – they offered to supply labour more cheaply than direct employment. Councils were given general encouragement to contract out services with Southend council leading the way with the privatisation of refuse collection in 1981. The net result of these pressures is to cheapen labour through the imposition of worse pay and conditions – a key function of the cuts.

In general, the Tories have been ruthlessly committed to encouraging recession as a way of resolving the problems of industry. Instead of Labour's policy of simply abandoning full employment as an objective and using incomes policies to cut personal income, they have simply allowed closures, bankruptcies and soaring unemployment to act as the most vicious kind of incomes policy and to generate its consequential leap in productivity. Similar circumstances were forced on the nationalised industries by the more stringent use of cash limits on their ability to borrow money.

Reactions to these policies have been mixed. The CBI, whose member firms include those suffering from the recession as well as the more successful ones, was divided in its response, but after internal rows early in the government's period of office maintained a position of support, with some reservations. The City remained consistently happy with the policies being pursued, even when the government effectively abandoned its commitment to a money supply target at the end of 1981. By then, the CBI, the City and the government were agreed that the reduction in interest rates was a higher priority, and thus the obsession with the money supply was dropped from being the sole policy issue – on the understanding that the basic aims of curbing public spending remained unchanged.

Unions – splits and struggles

The issue of cuts brought about a major split within the trade union movement in the mid-1970s. The TUC establishment supported a strategy that claimed to be boosting industrial prosperity and employment,. Out of a sense of loyalty to Labour ministers, and a barely suppressed view that public servants were too numerous, too pampered, and not real workers, the TUC offered no real opposition to the cuts policy. It was an open secret that many leading figures, like Hugh Scanlon of the AUEW, positively welcomed the cuts. In almost Thatcherite language, the TUC declared that it fully recognised that 'it would be wrong to treat the public sector as a bottomless purse'.

The public service unions, some of which were recent affiliates to the TUC and without Labour Party links, felt differently. Although the 1975 Congress carried a NALGO motion declaring that any further cuts would be regarded as a 'fundamental breach of the social contract', it was clear that the TUC establishment would not lead any public campaign against government policy. A separate body was set up, the National Steering Committee against the Cuts, comprising nearly all the major public service unions. The exceptions were the GMWU and the TGWU, which had largely industrial memberships, were at the centre of the TUC establishment, and were Labour loyalists. The steering committee organised a demonstration in November 1976, with over 60,000 people, an unprecedented figure for a weekday, which was largely ignored by the media and by the non-participant TUC.

At local level, joint union campaigns were set up, and in a number of areas active opposition was organised by local community groups. Hospital closures and cuts were a focus of especially strong, organised opposition. The pattern of co-ordinated action by public service unions, local campaigning, and TUC tacit support for the government remained basically unchanged until the general election of 1979.

While the cuts were the primary union issue from 1975 to 1977, battles over pay later became the focus, with the Fire Brigades Union fighting and winning the first pay dispute at the end of 1977, and council workers, health workers and civil servants taking on the government in 1978–79. In none of these disputes did the TUC give whole-hearted backing to the unions involved. It actually threatened the civil service unions with disciplinary action by the TUC unless they called off their strike in 1979 and accepted the government's offer. Meanwhile, the establishment groups of the police, the armed forces, doctors and dentists, and top judges and functionaries, had been awarded special case increases well in excess of the pay policy which workers were still expected to observe.

The experience of these years led to a sharp politicisation of public service workers. The traditional distinction between union activity over jobs and pay, and political activity centred round support for the Labour Party, could not be maintained. Attacks on these workers were a central part of a political programme being carried out by a Labour government, and defence of public services was a direct challenge to the parliamentary consensus. The political issues raised by fighting the cuts were more fundamental than the traditional union and Labour party activities enshrined in the 'social contract'.

The response to the Tory government reflected the earlier splits. Workers and community groups continued to fight and campaign against cuts as they had for the previous four years. A number of major battles were fought over pay by steel workers, civil servants and health workers. Local action against cuts and privatisation was taken in a number of councils.

The TUC formally opposed the policies of Tory cuts, but in May 1980 it consciously shied away from organising full-blooded industrial action against government policies. Most effort by the Labour establishment was devoted to 'broad' campaigns, such as that led by local authority associations against some government proposals for curbing councils' financial freedom – with some degree of success due to parliamentary support from Tory 'wets'.

One major response from the Labour Party, the TUC and some sections of the left has been the construction of an 'Alternative Economic Strategy' (AES) based on the expectation of a future Labour government reversing current policies by pursuing such a strategy. The 'traditional' form of Labour politics is thus preserved, despite the lessons of 1974–79; and the AES itself does little to enshrine public services at the centre of a socialist strategy (as Chapter 8 argues in detail.

It is worth remembering that the Labour government fell in 1979 amidst a final outbreak of resistance from public service unions over pay. That government's final stand was in defence of administratively imposed cash limits against some of the lowest paid workers in the country. Labour ministers proclaimed the irresponsibility of jeopardising public services through strike action, while the TUC devoted its efforts to leaning on unions to give in and accept the government's offer, and advising member unions that picket lines need not be observed.

Summary

The hostility to public services shown over the period since 1974 has been a systematic expression of the supremacy of production for profit over collective provision for social use. It has not been a matter of party politics – a Labour government, with the only slightly reluctant approval of the TUC, blazed the trail which the Tories followed. The machinery for delivering cuts has been strengthened over this period, and is now a powerful part of the structure of Britain, with a political impetus of its own.

The following six chapters analyse the key components of this machine. Chapter 2 deals with the way the very basis of economic accounting is loaded against public services. Chapters 3 and 4 analyse the way the systems of taxation and borrowing operate to ensure that the demands of business profitability get priority. Chapters 5 and 6 look at the network of controls which strangle political pressures for better public services. Chapter 7 looks at how the workers involved in collective care are systematically squeezed as a burden to business. The last two chapters examine how alternative strategies advocated by the left fail to alter this structure, and set out some of the political demands involved in changing it. Machinery dealing with the businessperson's problem of public spending needs to be replaced by machinery which can process socialist demands for public services.

2.

How the Sums are Loaded

Public services matter to people. But public spending is a problem for a capitalist economy. The government use economic definitions and accountancy practices which highlight the problems for capitalism fairly well. They do not, however, reflect the importance of public services to people. Nor do they even set out the conflict of interests.

This accounting system is not just economically lopsided. It also imparts an insidious bias to political debate, and to the political decision-making processes. It is the technical framework of the cuts machine. This chapter looks at some of the major accountancy distortions, and makes some suggestions for correcting them.

Valueless services

In an important sense, public services are officially treated as having no value whatsoever. This is not just the opinion of the right wing of the Tory party, but is implicit in the country's National Accounts and in the government's annual public spending plans. The reason is that the value of the output of an industry is measured in economic terms by the value of its sales – and it is a politically important feature of public services that they are not sold to consumers.

One result of this convention is that the activity of the public services is treated simply as public *spending*. The plans and discussions about this part of the economy thus talk about only one side of the theoretical balance sheet – the costs. There are no corresponding benefits set out in equivalent money terms, as there are in the accounts of a company. Public spending appears as so much unproductive pocket money.

This kind of accountancy convention accurately reflects an economy which is based on production for profit. It is worth producing tanks, or running advertising campaigns, because companies make money out of the process, whereas care for the elderly is worthless. Women's traditional domestic work of unpaid caring is another example of services which are given no value.

The paper work of public accountancy does more than just reflect the way a capitalist economy is structured. It also shapes political arguments about how the economy should be organised. It makes it easier for politicians and the media to argue or assume that public spending is wasteful, because there is no clear monetary gain from it. It makes arguments that public services are a parasitic burden on the rest of the economy, seem more convincing. As long as the basis of discussion is the cost of public spending, it makes it difficult for socialists to argue for improving and extending public services.

One extreme example of this loaded accountancy is in the new presentation of public spending in terms of 'cash'. Only the actual money spent each year is set out, with no adjustment for inflation or anything else. Nothing appears except the costs. Under the system which operated until 1981, spending plans were set out in constant prices adjusted for inflation, which were treated as giving a rough measure of the volume of labour and other resources put into public services (for a fuller account of these systems see Chapter 5). This 'volume' of spending was frequently regarded as a kind of proxy indication of the output of services.

But even this earlier method was only a weak substitute for assessing output. It could not compare the level of services with the need for them, it could not distinguish changes in resources from changes in the efficiency or quality of services, it did not assess the value of services or goods received in exchange for contracts with private companies, and it did not assess the value of collective public provision of services compared with leaving them to be dealt with by the private sector. 'Volume' plans were always primarily a way of measuring spending, which was their central role in planning.

Other conventional methods of measuring output are also inadequate. In the National Accounts, it is simply assumed that the output of most public services is proportionate to the numbers employed, or, in the case of the NHS, to the real wage bill. One silly result is that when governments claim to improve the productivity of public employees, the National Accounts solemnly record a relative drop in output! Other attempts to measure the product of public services are made by administrators – usually, ironically, to try and measure the efficiency of workers, which the National Accounts are adamant cannot change. Such administrative measures are invariably useless for actually establishing how good services are. For instance, a popular ratio with those checking on the social security system is the number of claimants dealt with per worker in social security offices. The most cursory discussion with either workers or claimants establishes that this tells you little about the level of service – about who should be getting benefits, about the way claimants should be treated, or about how complex the system should be (though it may reveal a lot about the pressure on workers). Another example is one of the administrators' criteria used in the NHS – the level of bed occupancy, i.e. how much of the time a hospital bed is filled by a patient. A simple way of improving this ratio is just to cut the number of beds, so that there are always patients desperately needing to fill them. This might be a great way to get the most out of a bed, but it is not what most people would regard as an improvement in health services.

Another possible method, which is rarely used, would be to value public services by what they would cost at market prices. Education might be valued by using the fees of non-boarding private schools as a guide, and comparing the cost per pupil of state education. On this basis, the output of the primary and secondary education services in 1981 was worth about 1½ times the cost of providing those services. Such an approach would not only be of limited application, however, but would also involve accepting that market value is the proper way of assessing public services – a type of argument that few socialists would accept.

Politics, then, are central to this issue of valuation. One of the unfortunate features of Keynesian economics, which is generally in favour of public 'spending' as a way of stimulating economic growth, is that it fails to challenge the establishment assumption that it is the *level* of spending which matters and not the services. This is one of the reasons why the Alternative Economic Strategy, discussed in more detail in Chapter 7, does not provide an adequate *political* programme for public services. Such a political programme needs to be firmly based on how workers and users value the services they get – or don't get. This kind of political evaluation may not be easy to assimilate into conventional economic accounting, but it is more important to get the politics right than to cramp them within an accountancy straitjacket.

The unproductive luxury of jobs

It remains a firm principle of government that state-sector jobs are a luxury that the public can scarcely afford. The level of unemployment makes no difference to this rule, which is another result of treating public spending solely as a cost. The wages bill is just another, particularly large, cost item. In public spending plans, wages are treated exactly like unemployment benefit, except that wages are somewhat higher. It is therefore more cost-effective to reduce the number of public service jobs than to reduce unemployment.

The logic of this perverse arithmetic affects a lot of discussion about public service jobs. One point which is often made about unemployment is that it costs the state almost as much in benefits and lost taxation as it would to employ people. This perfectly accurate observation, however, fails to challenge the official assumption that jobs and unemployment can be fairly evaluated by comparing their costs in terms of public spending. The danger is in implicitly accepting the conclusion – which some Tories draw explicitly – that public service jobs are only worth having if the level of wages makes them no more expensive than unemployment.

What is even more remarkable is that both the Labour government of 1974–79 and the subsequent Tory government have proudly accepted this accountancy practice as the basis for a public commitment to targets for destroying jobs. The media have urged them on in this, and produced harsh criticism whenever the politicians appeared to be falling behind in their objectives.

Treating jobs as a cost is of course the practice adopted in the private sector as well. But public employees are also treated by the Treasury as never improving their productivity at all. This is not done on the basis of careful observation of the immutable idleness of public servants, but is purely an accounting convention to decide what the figures should be.

Thus in the National Accounts, as already mentioned, the output of services is assumed to be proportionate to the numbers employed, and so by definition a given number of workers can never change their output. When public spending plans were drawn up using constant prices, it was explicitly assumed that public employees never improved their productivity. Since other workers in the economy demonstrably were improving their productivity, this led automatically to the result that the labour costs of public services rose faster than in the private sector, if wage rates rose at the same speed. This was called the 'Relative Price Effect', and is often referred to as the reason why the costs of public services are dangerously uncontrollable.

This result is simply the product of an arbitrary accounting assumption, and yet politicians, the media and academics usually talk as though it was a fact of life. It has been of considerable influence in supporting the view that it is inflationary to keep public employees' pay rising in line with private sector earnings, because their productivity is supposed not to rise.

The assumption is false as well as arbitrary. For instance, most manual workers for councils and hospitals are paid under productivity schemes where their output is regularly measured. If the Treasury were right, hundreds of work study officers would be regularly lying through their teeth.

The assumption also leads to distortions in the measurement of the growth of the economy by the Gross National Product. It would be perfectly possible to adopt a convention more in line with reality, that public service productivity rises at the same rate – or even half the rate – of workers in sectors with measured, marketed output, and to calculate Gross National Product accordingly.

These accounting practices make a real contribution to the politics of the treatment of public service workers. They reflect the fact that the cost of employing people who do not contribute directly to profitable production is a cost that private capital will want to reduce. But they obstruct political arguments for a programme of expanding employment and creating jobs in the public services, as well as the need for decent pay and conditions for workers. These issues are looked at in more detail in Chapter 7.

Magic savings

Public spending plans consistently claim to perform economic magic by 'saving' money from nowhere. Cuts in services, jobs or benefits appear simply as so many millions of pounds saved. Politicians are clearly captivated by this wonderful phenomenon, and announce such 'savings' as though they were the proud directors of a company making record profits.

This illusion is possible only because Treasury accounting ignores most of the economic effects. Unless the savings are unscrambled so that we can see where the money is coming from and going to, a sensible political evaluation is almost impossible. Costs do not disappear, they are redistributed and borne by different groups of people. Two examples are unscrambled here, to prove that money does not grow out of Treasury biros.

Take first the announcement in the 1976 White Paper that – among many other cuts – 'the government intends to save an additional £140 million by reductions in planned expenditure on staff'. This meant scrapping 38,000 civil service jobs. All that appeared in the tables of the White Paper was a little entry: '−£140 million'.

Where does this 'saving' come from? The White Paper does not spell it out. The source is the loss of income and employment by 38,000 people who do not have jobs as a result. And who gets this 'saving'? The answer, which again is not spelt out in the White Paper, is that taxation and borrowing is reduced – and who benefits from that is looked at in detail in the next two chapters. So what masquerades as a simple 'saving' by the government turns out to be a transaction in which a large group of people are forced to give up their prospective jobs so that taxpayers and financiers can have an extra £140 million to play with in whatever way they like (the White Paper does no more than guess at how they might use this windfall).

The process thus has two sides, but the Treasury acts as the accountant only for the taxpayers and financiers. And there are further factors involved, which are not mentioned by the Treasury's presentation. The unemployed workers are likely to make some smaller additional demand on finances because of extra benefits and lost taxes. There are also unquantifiable but real factors on both sides: workers in general will suffer the disadvantages of a tighter labour market, while employers and their financiers will enjoy a corresponding gain. Those still working will probably find themselves increasing their workload to compensate for the absent workers. Users of the services will probably get a worse deal too.

A similar analysis can be made of the 'savings' made by increasing charges. In the 1980 White Paper, for example, it was decided that council rents should be increased by £2.10 per week, and that school meals should cost more. These measures were claimed to 'save' about £200 million per year.

Neither measure, however, had any effect on the cost of providing school meals or council housing. The gain from these changes is once again a reduction in the burden of finance on taxpayers and financiers – but the money comes from tenants and parents shelling out an extra £200 million from their own pockets. Again, there are other factors: there will probably be some increased entitlement to social security as a result, thus slightly off-setting the gains and losses (say 10 per cent of the total). Moreover, the higher prices for meals will force some families into substituting for school meals – e.g. by preparing sandwiches, increasing the load on unpaid domestic labour and worsening children's nutrition.

Other changes in public spending can be analysed in the same way – changes in benefits, real pay, current services, and even capital spending. In all cases, the official figure-work considers only the economic gains to taxpayers and financiers. For political reactionaries, this is an adequate system of accounting. For socialists, it is hopelessly lopsided. This kind of imbalance recurs in other aspects of the cuts machine – Chapter 3, for example, looks at the differences in the treatment of tax reliefs and social security benefits.

Another remarkable aspect of government assessment of public services is that, whereas public spending costs money, private spending does not. This is partly because the accounting is so lopsided that it does not show burdens being transferred onto people, and also because public spending is conventionally defined as being net of any charges made on the consumer. As a result, increasing the amount parents have to pay towards school meals appears as a reduction in public spending, but not as an increase in private spending.

This is patently ludicrous. Paying fares costs money just the same as paying rates; higher rents are an extra expense just as higher taxes are; private education is not free. The most graphic illustration is the case of health services. The more we pay for the NHS by way of fees and charges, the less the NHS costs, according to the Treasury's figurework. If we paid higher and higher charges for drugs, and paid for occupying hospital beds, and so on, the health service would appear in the accounts as costing 'the country' less and less. The ultimate saving, from the Treasury's point of view, would be if we got rid of the NHS altogether and threw ourselves on the mercy of private enterprise. The government's plans would proudly show that health care was no longer a burden to the nation, and the country would have 'saved' £15 billion per year. This claim would be unaffected by the fact that such a system in the USA consumes a much higher percentage of national income, and is less comprehensive, less fair and less efficient than the NHS.

A similar absurdity is apparent in the treatment of borrowing by industries to finance investment. If a nationalised industry borrows money, the government accounts treat it as costing 'the country' the amount borrowed: if the same industry were denationalised, and borrowed the same amount for the same kind of investment, it would not appear as costing the country anything. If both were treated as making equal demands on the country's resources, it is unlikely that there would have been so much delight at the plans of Barclays Bank and others to spend millions of pounds building a second telephone system. It would quite rightly be regarded as an incredible waste.

These points would have been more like illustrations of possible absurd consequences of accounting principles, until the Tory cabinet in 1982 received a paper from the government's think-tank which seriously argued for just such extreme conclusions. The abolition of the NHS was the centrepiece of their suggestions for dealing with the problem of public spending. The insidious political bias of present accounting practices could not have been more sharply illustrated.

What can be afforded

All these features of the accounts mean that the terms in which public services are planned are heavily loaded from the outset. Services are without independent value, jobs are an unproductive burden, and the figures present the implications only in terms of the need for financing by taxes or borrowing.

It is thus not surprising that the constant theme of discussions about public spending is 'what the country can afford'. But this phrase simply identifies 'the country' with the private sector, and 'what can be afforded' with the amount spent on public services. This is not a recent innovation of a Tory government obsessed with monetarist theories. The same image was at the heart of the system of planning the 'mixed economy' in the 1950s and 1960s. Thus the Labour government in 1969 reaffirmed the view of its predecessor that public spending plans needed to be assessed 'by what they imply in use of currently produced resources: this would give a broad indication of what would have to be currently foregone in the rest of the economy'.

The glaring political problem with this type of planning is that the government, by definition, does not control the private sector's allocation of resources. Thus although the plans set out the financial requirements of public spending on the health service, they do not set out the financial requirements of company spending on advertising, or of personal spending on works of art and jewellery. And yet these categories of spending equally imply that resources are foregone by other parts of the economy – like the health service. The whole process is lopsided. The sector of the economy which is under government control is planned so as to fit in with the needs of the uncontrolled and unplanned sector.

The perfect example of the consequences of this approach was the 1976 White Paper on public spending. Faced with inflation and recession, the government cut the plans for public services in later years, declaring:

> When world demand picks up, more resources will be needed for export and investment. We must ensure they are available for that purpose. Unless we are prepared to see rising taxation reduce takehome pay, these resources can be made available only if we keep public expenditure at roughly the same level for several years. Changing the structural distribution of resources in this way is the only means of restoring and maintaining full employment.

The government could, and did, ensure that resources were cut from public services – including investment programmes. But it could only hope, guess, and forecast that the private sector would take up those resources and use them for the desired ends. There could not be spending plans for the whole economy. The other aspect of these decisions, however, was an effective political decision to alter the allocation of income and control of economic resources. Switching resources to industry was done mainly by increasing the income taken by companies in the form of profits, which are both the main source of funds for, and the main incentive for, investment. Although the spending of the private sector could not be effectively determined, its income could be.

Why public spending?

Perhaps the most general problem is the very use of 'public spending' as a category for planning and discussion. By contrast with the term 'public services', it focuses on the costs to capitalism rather than the benefits to people. It is a measure of what has to be financed out of taxation and borrowing – and even these categories are defined in a politically loaded way, as the following two chapters show.

The term embraces politically different categories, like defence and social services. It lumps together economically disparate items, like spending on goods and services, transfer payments and capital investment on roads and housing. It does not even measure spending, since it is presented net of rents and charges.

As the Tory government has demonstrated, it is perfectly possible to restructure the accounting of the public services as a political tool. Similar political possibilities would be open to a left government. To start with, transfer payments could be simply removed from the whole exercise, and dealt with as part of the budget presentation, which would then provide a fuller picture of the government's intervention in the distribution of income. Defence and law and order could become the subject of an entirely separate exercise, with a different publication and timescale. Social services and government administration could then be the subject of detailed consultative and final planning documents, setting out the services to be provided, the amount to be spent, charges shown separately, and the taxation implications of each service. The simple arithmetical exercise of totalling the sums to work out the borrowing requirement could continue, without the necessity to formally reduce every public service into the format required for this calculation. It would even be possible to set alongside the plans for social services the historic and expected expenditure on items such as advertising, so that the issue of 'resources foregone' should be capable of discussion in both directions. And so on.

Summary

The political bias in the figures is a problem to be recognised. Apparently straightforward lists of figures conceal a political balance sheet with different classes on different sides. References to the 'country' and the 'economy' refer to the interests of a particular section of the economy – a section which is not publicly controlled, but to whose interest the government-run sector is subordinated.

The accounting system itself creates some political disadvantages for socialists. It is technically possible to make changes which would alter this to some extent, mainly by forcing the presentation to reflect the class divisions more clearly. Socialist responses to attacks on public services, in any case, need to challenge the presentation bias, or risk fighting under rules which are heavily weighted against public service and workers.

Changing the accounting system does not, however, change society: the hard cash values of business transactions remain dominant. By contrast, socialist politics demand that services and the rest of economic activity should be valued and controlled by the workers and communities involved. The value of public services is thus a central political issue.

3.

The Shifting Burden of Taxation

In the mid-1970s Denis Healey was fond of justifying his cuts in public services by saying that the people he drank with in Leeds did not want to pay higher taxes. It would have been startling if anyone who found themselves drinking with a Chancellor of the Exchequer expressed a desire to pay more tax. This kind of appeal to the 'taxpayer' is used not only by politicians, but by academics, too, as the reason why public spending must be curbed.

Asking if people want services cut to pay for their tax reductions usually produces rather different answers. Even the wealthy citizens of California, who voted for a constitutional amendment to cut taxes and are held up as a model by right-wing economists, subsequently said they did not want public services reduced. The demand for lower taxation fades a little if the positive value of services is presented. It remains, however, a powerful weapon of political reaction.

A closer look at the tax system shows that there is not just an undifferentiated mass of 'taxpayers' who share a common interest. Those who have most income and wealth to start with stand to gain most from hanging on to it. Those with incomes so low that they are not taxable stand to gain nothing from cuts in income tax. The way the system operates makes it even easier for powerful political and economic interests to keep their own taxes low at the expense of the rest of us. Local taxes – the rates – break down in the same way; there is a divergence of interest between those who own property and those who don't. Taxes and rates do impose an unfair burden on the poor

– not because public services are an intolerable burden but because of the way the system protects the rich.

Relief for the rich

One outstanding example of how the tax system protects those with money is the vast structure of tax reliefs. There are a great number of these, only a very few of which affect most of us. The great majority apply only to businesses or the wealthy – like the relief on companies' investment or the reliefs on transfers of capital. They are not publicised as being a burden to society, but they have the same effect as state grants. In fact, in the 1970s, investment grants to companies (which appeared as public spending) were replaced by tax reliefs, and child tax allowances were replaced by child benefits.

As a result, there is a distortion in the way that government grants are perceived. The benefits paid to the poor are seen as large amounts spent by society, whereas tax reliefs are not publicly discussed every year – although the rest of us have to pay for them in the same way.

If all government grants and tax reliefs are counted together, an unusual picture is revealed (see Table 3, p. 109). Private business turns out to be much the biggest beneficiary, receiving over £13,000 million in 1980–81 – over four times as much as the total support to nationalised industries. The council tenant is well down the list, with £2,250 million, far below the £5,350 million given to houseowners, and below those wealthy enough to pick up the £3,500 million relief on their capital gains and transfers. Married men are well treated, too, with £3,030 million of special relief – not far below the total benefits and reliefs of £4,680 million that women and children had to share.

These figures highlight the obvious fact that tax reliefs do most for those who have most to start with. They treat the rich as entitled to keep what they have, even at the expense of the rest of us. The administration of the tax and social security systems operates on the same principle. Tax avoidance is regarded as legitimate, and even illegal tax evasion is not exactly hotly pursued. The Inland Revenue devotes comparatively few resources to chasing the businesses who hijack enormous sums from the exchequer by tax fiddles, yet the social security system devotes an increasing proportion of its effort to harassing claimants who get more than the tiny sums they are entitled to under current laws. It makes no economic sense – the government stands to make far more from catching tax evaders than it does from stopping social security fiddles. It just makes sense as a political bias against the poor.

The strongest opponents of taxation are the rich. The last thing they want is for it to remove some of their wealth. The distribution of wealth and income is grossly unequal before taxes make any impact. In 1980, nearly one-third of Britain's domestic income was taken by profits, rent and small businesses – the rest was shared out among employed workers. In the mid-1970s, the top 10 per cent had more income than the bottom 50 per cent and more wealth than the rest of us put together. This enormous concentration of economic power resists attempts to spread it by taxation.

One way it's done is by heavy political pressure. The Labour government abandoned its plans for a tax on wealth, in 1976, after massive lobbying from those threatened. Yet the proposed tax would have had only a modest effect, and only on the wealthiest 5 per cent in the country. In 1974, and again in 1982, multinational companies successfully persuaded two different Chancellors of the Exchequer not to bring in tax measures which would have limited their ability to avoid tax by shifting funds from one country to another. They were treated rather differently from the rest of us, too. In 1982, the Treasury considerately circulated their proposals to companies, for their comments, some months before the budget.

By contrast, in 1976 and 1977 the Treasury offered some slight general reduction in income tax only on condition that workers agreed to pay restraint. The unemployed, who were told in 1980 that the value of benefits would be cut by 5 per cent, as an interim measure until benefit was made taxable, found in 1982 that their benefit was being taxed and they had not got back their 5 per cent. If companies had been treated like that there would be uproar.

Another way that those with money get rid of their tax burden is by using their economic power. Flows of unearned income can be transformed by accountants into capital gains (which are taxed more lightly), or 'hidden' in the retained earnings on a company's profit and loss account, or frozen out of reach of taxes in assets like land. Other favoured tax shelters are insurance policies, family trusts and farms, all of which get favoured treatment from the Inland Revenue. The value remains the same, but far less tax is paid.

An even simpler way that businesses have of getting rid of their tax liabilites is to just pass on the bill to the rest of us by increasing their prices. This was officially accepted in the price controls operated in the early 1970s, which explicitly allowed companies to raise prices to cover any rate increases that they had to pay.

Organised workers can seek to respond in kind, by pushing for pay increases from companies to cover increased taxes on their earnings. This kind of pressure caused alarm in the mid-1970s, because it was said to be inflationary for workers to try and do what companies were officially allowed to do. Under the social contract, the TUC even put out a circular warning trade unionists not to make such pay claims.

But the majority of the population – the unemployed, children, pensioners and others dependent on benefits – have no effective way of 'passing on' their costs. Their income depends solely on political demands for higher public spending on benefits. Tax reductions have virtually no effect on their welfare at all.

Carrying the load

It is not surprising that the load of taxation has come to fall increasingly heavily on workers. Companies proved so successful at shedding their tax burden that by 1979 they were paying only 8 per cent of total taxes, compared with over 18 per cent in 1946. Indeed, in the tax year 1978–79 the 20 biggest UK companies were paying virtually no corporation tax at all. The rest of us were paying more instead.

The tax system itself helps to put the load onto workers. National Insurance contributions have increased a lot in recent years, and account for a higher percentage of all taxes; and they are a tax which is loaded most heavily onto the poor. They are paid only by workers, not by those on unearned income, and they are paid only on income *below* a certain limit. As a result, the better-off actually pay a lower percentage of their income in National Insurance than the rest of us.

Budget changes in recent years, especially under the Tory government, have accelerated the effect further. Although the 1979 budget, for example, claimed proudly to have reduced everyone's income tax by cutting the basic rate from 33 per cent to 30 per cent, it actually increased the total taxes paid by people in general, mainly because VAT was massively increased. As Table 4 (p. 110) shows, the first four Tory budgets, in the period 1979–82, had the effect of increasing the burden on people in general by nearly £2,100 million per year, while reducing the taxes paid on companies, holders of capital, and the highest incomes by about £3,400 million.

This immense transfer of the burden of taxation is obscured by the usual way budgets are discussed, which concentrates on the changes in income tax rates and the overall effect of the budget on the government's revenue. In 1979, not only was the income tax 'concession' wiped out by the VAT increases; the overall effect of an increase in taxes of £400 million obscured the fact that companies, capital and the rich got a tax *cut* of £600 million – and the rest of us had to pay an extra £1,000 million.

Political resistance by the rich to taxation eroding their money has been remarkably successful. The tax system does not redistribute income very effectively. In 1976–77 the poorest 50 per cent of the population started with 24.1 per cent of all income before tax, and after taxation had reduced everyone's income they had progressed to having 26.9 per cent. The top 10 per cent started with 26.2 per cent of income, and after tax they still had 23.2 per cent. This was not an accident, a law of economics, or divine intervention. It was their reward for persistent and ruthless political struggle over the taxation system to ensure it favoured them.

Rates and class

Rates have become a very emotive issue in recent years. By mid-1982, the unions, local authorities, the Confederation of British Industry, the Labour Party, and in theory the Tory Party were all in favour of replacing rates wholly or partially by a local income tax. Their reasons differ, however. The Tories' attitude to the rates is refreshingly simple. They think that people in big comfortable residences should not have to pay rates to councils for running public services. The CBI's view is almost as simple – companies should not have to cut into their profits to pay for public services.

These views of the rich and powerful stem from different interests to the more widespread resentment of the rates system. This is based on the simple fact that they fall very unfairly between individuals. Two people with very different incomes may have to pay the same rates just because they happen to live in similar housing. Rates take a larger percentage of the income of ordinary people than of those who are better-off.

The unfairness between people tends to obscure the more general clash of interests over rates. Rates are a tax on the occupiers of certain sorts of property, and, because property ownership is very unevenly distributed, they might be expected to be a tax which hits the rich hardest. They don't, however, because the politics of the system has produced some major limitations on the rates.

First, some property is exempt from rates altogether. Since 1929, farmers have not paid rates on agricultural land, which is one of the many reasons why farmland has become a favourite investment. The Queen and the royal family are exempt from the obligation to pay any rates at all. In Scotland, only half the value of business property is rated. And companies throughout Britain are only rated on the value of their premises, not their machinery or stocks. Capital invested in shares or bonds or jewellery or old masters is not rated at all.

These exemptions mean that the burden of rates is concen-

trated on housing (and business premises). The second political
factor then comes into play. The rates are demanded not from
the owner of a property, but from the occupier, so that even
those who don't own their own house pay rates as though they
did. The state in effect assumes that any sensible landlord will
pass the cost onto the tenants anyway. The largest class
affected by this rule are council tenants. The net result of these
factors is that those who own virtually no wealth at all are
paying substantial rates, whereas those who own vast amounts
of concentrated wealth in the form of farmland, shares, etc., do
not pay rates on that wealth.

A recent academic work *Local Government Finance in a
Unitary State* has commented that 'the earliest protection of
the poor [from rates] was that the very poor lived in work-
houses and those that were less poor lived in very crowded
property of low value'. This golden age has now gone, and
nearly everyone lives in houses where they have to pay rates.

There is now a complex system of housing benefits and
governmental grants aimed at reducing the burden of rates on
householders. As part of the Rate Support Grant domestic rate
relief gives councils a fixed amount of money proportional to
the total rateable value of the houses in their area. This
obviously is of most benefit to councils in rich areas, with high
rateable values. Moreover, it is a fixed amount which has not
changed since 1975, whereas the rates have gone up since that
time. So the proportion of total rates paid by people in houses
has risen steadily, whereas business rates have contributed a
declining percentage of the total.

All this complex system of rate relief to individuals was
worth about £1,400 million in 1981–82. Companies, on the
other hand, with no trouble or public fuss, are able to set their
rate payments against their tax – unlike individuals. With the
rate of corporation tax at 52 per cent (in theory), this concession could have been worth £3,000 million in the same year.

As with national taxes, the balance of the burden of rates is
loaded heavily by political features of the system, and the
concessions to business are concealed. Even so, businesses pay
a much higher percentage of rates than they do of national

taxes: commercial and industrial premises paid about 39 per cent of all rates in 1981–82, compared with only 18 per cent of all taxes, including National Insurance contributions, in 1979. In terms of the distribution of taxes between classes, therefore, it would be a backward step to scrap rates in favour of general taxes on income. Instead, a political offensive to remove the exemptions of agricultural and crown property, to extend the range of property subject to rates, and to remove rates altogether from those who don't own property, would strengthen the position of the working class as a whole and those worst affected by the current unfair system. Rates are the nearest to a potential real wealth tax that exists. It would be a shame to see them abandoned simply because the battles between classes over their distribution have been fought hardest by capital.

Taxpayers' democracy

Taxation is not only political: it is frequently talked of as though it was the basis of democracy. It is often argued that the political accountability of local councils depends upon their powers of taxation, and hence it is 'the ratepayers' to whom councils are accountable. On this basis, some people argue for an extension of the taxation powers of councils, and the CBI argues that businesses should either not pay rates or be given extra 'business' votes.

It is important to spell out the political implications of this kind of argument. At present, all adults have the vote, regardless of whether they pay taxes or rates. That principle matters precisely because political decisions should not be restricted to those who have money, and because socialist politics involve demanding that those with money should lose the power that comes with it. In a 'ratepayers' democracy', political power is only legitimate for those with enough money to want to keep it out of public control. It is worth remembering that businesspeople had two votes – one as householders and one as business owners – until 1969: the last relic of the old pattern of government which limited the vote to property-owners.

The issue is not just abstract, or a harmless nuance of academic debate. As Chapter 6 shows, recent decisions of the highest courts in the land have effectively ruled that councils must operate in the interests of the ratepayer, whatever the electorate may wish. As Chapter 5 shows, the principle that parliament must give overriding protection to the interests of taxpayers seriously distorts the parliamentary approach to public services.

Summary

The interests of the 'taxpayer' which are supposed to limit public spending turn out to be class interests. Those with economic power use political pressures, and the structure of the tax system, to protect their interests. The conflict between public services and the reluctant taxpayers is a real one, but it is a political conflict over whether resources should be controlled and allocated by collective democratic decisions, or by the class which controls them now by virtue of its power.

Socialists don't have to accept the simple Tory slogan that 'you're either for the taxpayers or against them'. The burden of tax on workers and the poor is a real issue, but can be faced on the basis of a political analysis of the taxation system. The further point has to be faced that profit-starved capital has a real problem with the burden of taxation. It needs the rest of us to carry an increasingly large share of it, or to reduce the total by cuts in services, and is prepared to fight for that.

4.

Borrowing in Confidence

Government borrowing is surrounded by a great mystique. Newspapers and television solemnly announce the latest figures on the subject, which are taken as being enormously important. No one actually likes to show their ignorance by asking why, although hardly anybody talked about the public sector borrowing requirement (PSBR) before 1975. Apart from pure mystique, it is also a technically difficult subject.

But behind the mystique and the technicalities lies a highly political process. Just as 'the taxpayers' interests' conceal a set of class conflicts over control of economic resources, so government borrowing is tied up with the politics of financial capital. This was brought home to Britain in 1976, when the financiers insisted that a whole set of policies should be adopted before the confidence of the money markets was restored. The same phenomenon was apparent in 1982, when discussions over a loan to Mexico were halted for days, simply because the new head of Mexico's main bank was a man with an economics degree from Cambridge, and thus regarded as a dangerously communistic influence.

This chapter looks at some aspects of government borrowing, and tries to do two things. First, to show that the mystique of the figures can be unwrapped to show political forces. Second, to show that it is more the purposes of government borrowing than its scale that determines its political acceptability to financiers.

Real borrowing

As a preliminary, it is worth discussing the whole idea of borrowing. To hear some commentators talk, you would think that borrowing was the biggest economic sin. Yet virtually everyone borrows at some time – mortgages to buy a house, or hire purchase to buy other goods. Most of all, companies borrow: in 1981, for example, industrial and commercial companies raised £11 billion by borrowing from banks and others – the same as the whole public sector. Yet there is never any public alarm at the level of the corporate sector borrowing requirement.

The crucial difference is of course the purpose for which money is borrowed. Companies raise loans to finance productive and profitable activities, whereas the government finances public spending which is regarded, as shown in Chapter 2, as wasteful consumption. The public sector borrowing requirement (PSBR), the difference between the amount spent on public services and the amount collected from taxes and charges, is thus carefully scrutinised by financiers. An increase is viewed with deep suspicion.

Yet the government is not taking on an intolerable financial burden by borrowing. In real terms, it has gained money steadily by doing so: 'The broad picture is that over the whole postwar period the real PSBR has almost invariably been in surplus.' This statement by the Treasury in April 1982 is somewhat at odds with the regular reports of the awesome cost to the government of borrowing. It reflects the simple fact that the money borrowed by the government (or anyone else) is worth less when it is finally repaid than it was when it was borrowed. On a personal level, this fact is well known to those who buy their own houses with a mortgage: as the months and years go by and inflation proceeds, the repayments become less and less costly in real terms.

The same is true on a larger scale for major borrowers like the government. The £5,000 million that was borrowed in 1970 was worth a lot less when it was repaid in 1980: about a quarter, in fact. So while the government paid interest on those loans for 10 years, it gained from the erosion of the value of its debt. Since the government is constantly borrowing and repaying money, this kind of gain has been continual.

So, according to the Bank of England, all the public sector borrowing during the period of supposed profligacy from 1973 to 1978 was more than offset by a fall in the value of government debts, and so the real PSBR was a surplus of about £600 million per year (see Table 5, p. 110).

Similarly, the company sector, whose financial troubles were treated as such a serious problem in the mid-1970s, with a financial deficit of £3.9 billion over the years 1973–75, actually gained £7.1 billion in those same years from the erosion of the value of its debts. The real gain was over £3 billion. Other sectors of the economy lost from this process. Overseas lenders lost about £800 million per year in value during the 1970s. Another loser was the personal sector, whose savings are the ultimate source of most finance for companies and government: the value of these savings was eroded fastest of all during the 1970s. The problem with the PSBR has thus had little to do with its cost to the government, which, like houseowners and companies, has continued to make a steady profit on its borrowing over the years. Indeed, in 1975 the national debt was a smaller proportion of Gross National Product than it had been in 1875, was lower than at any time since the first world war, and had been declining sharply ever since the end of the second world war. Britain's outstanding national debt, in real terms, *fell* by 23 per cent during the 1970s: a period when the real national debts of the USA, West Germany and Japan *rose* by 14 per cent, 107 per cent, and 35 per cent respectively.

Nor is this point simply an abstruse economic fact. The largest part of the costs of council housing is interest payments: more or less the whole of the rents paid by council tenants is swallowed by this charge. And yet the *real* cost to councils of this continuing borrowing to finance housing is negative: it is not a real cost at all. If housing revenue accounts were adjusted to reflect this real borrowing cost, then rents and rates could be massively reduced at the stroke of an accountant's pen. If this seems a ludicrous idea, it is only what happened to businesses in 1974. A simple accounting change, which ruled that the profits in the increased value of company stock were not real profits for tax purposes, gave them an instant windfall of 3½ per cent of national income: and accountants have been debating various forms of accounting for companies which would allow for inflation ever since. At the moment, council tenants are paying for the steady reduction of the national debt. It would be quite possible to reverse this situation by a simple political decision.

This point about the real cost of borrowing is more relevant than most of the mystical utterances about public borrowing. One such utterance was the forecast of the PSBR used by the Treasury in 1976 as a reason for making swingeing cuts: it was wrong by as much as the cuts themselves, and was widely seen to be wrong at the time by others, including Britain's Common Market partners. Yet that forecast remained at the centre of policy argument, as though the level of the PSBR had to be talked into being unacceptably high even if it wasn't really. Another untruth is the persistent presumption that the PSBR is the biggest influence on the money supply – the total amount of money and credit in the economy. It is not, and has not been for at least a decade, except for one very exceptional year in 1975. None of this, however, has prevented financiers from losing confidence at crucial points. Equally, in 1981, when they might have been expected to panic because of soaring money supply figures and the tacit abandonment of money supply targets, their confidence remained firm. It was not the technical practice that mattered, but whether the government was still pursuing their sort of policies. In 1976, a Labour government had to go a long way before financiers were satisfied that it was after all a government they could trust. In 1981, their confidence was unshaken by temporary adjustments. An examination of the way it all works brings out this institutionalised policy mechanism.

The dealers

The actual mechanics of public borrowing involve a very small group of people, subject to little direct political control, operating in the City. Parliament is not involved in any way: its authority is neither required nor sought for government borrowing. The key people are City financiers and Bank of England and Treasury officials. The latter decide on a daily and weekly basis how much to borrow and how to do it. Their information about the precise state of government spending and revenue comes from a handful of daily phone calls from government departments. The Bank of England, although technically a nationalised industry, is in practice even less politically controlled than other nationalised industries. Indeed, the City looks to the Bank of England to act as its spokesperson in any dealings with the government.

The cosiness of this relationship was illustrated during the civil service strike of 1981, when the government for 5 months had no clear knowledge of what it was spending and only a vague idea of the considerably reduced taxes it was collecting. Despite this uncertainty, the fact that the money supply was soaring, and the knowledge that large interest payments were being incurred by the government, the financial markets simply accepted the Bank of England's reassuring guesses at what was happening.

The borrowing itself is carried out in a number of ways. The first is issuing extra notes and coins, which is not so much a form of borrowing as literally printing money, reflecting the public's need for extra cash. This is almost an accidental source of finance for the government, because it has a monopoly on this activity. In recent years it has played a trivial role in financing the PSBR.

The second element is issuing gilts, which are government bonds of a fixed value sold on the market, with a promise to pay interest and a promise that the government will buy them back after a fixed time (e.g. 15 years). These are sold to banks, overseas investors, and above all to institutions like the pension funds and insurance companies. Gilts are much the most important form of government borrowing.

The third way is national savings, which are simply the government's way of borrowing the savings of individuals.

Since 1980, the government has consciously tried to increase the importance of national savings as a way of financing the PSBR.

The fourth way is the buying and selling of bills. The government issues Treasury bills – roughly like post-dated cheques – which are mainly bought by the banks. In recent years, however, the government has been buying back more Treasury bills than it has issued and so the effect of this operation has been to *increase* the amount the government has to borrow by other means. Companies also issue bills, and since 1980 the Bank of England has been a major buyer of such bills, so lending money to companies, and again *increasing* the borrowing needed from other sources.

The final element is borrowing from the banks. This is mainly done by local authorities rather than central government. Bank borrowing has been a relatively minor part of government finance in recent years and has usually been tiny by comparison with the amounts borrowed from the banks by the private sector.

Local authorities and nationalised industries' borrowing is also controlled by the government. Nationalised industries have limits set on the amount of money they are allowed to borrow, called External Financing Limits. Local authorities are only allowed to borrow for capital spending, and there are cash limits on the amount of capital spending they can undertake. Partly as a consequence, both groups tend to borrow most of their money from the government itself, which thus acts as the major borrowing agent for the whole public sector.

Public borrowing is thus not mainly a matter of printing money or running up overdrafts, but an operation involving the Bank of England dealing with pension funds, companies, overseas institutions and banks. The political pressures that this system can generate are enormous. And the PSBR itself is only *one* of the factors that influence these operations.

In 1980–81, for example, the PSBR was just over £13 billion. But the government bought back £1 billion of Treasury bills; lent £2 billion to companies by buying commercial bills; repaid nearly £1 billion of overseas loans; and repaid £3 billion of old debts. The key explanations for this 'over-funding' are monetary policy, the exchange rate and the confidence of financiers.

Helping financiers

The first major consideration is monetary policy. Since 1976, the financial markets, and hence governments, have been obsessed with controlling the money supply. Although the ways of measuring the money supply vary with academic fashion and political expediency, the crude principle is that it consists of notes and coins and credit – money in the pocket and in the chequebook. So it includes bank loans to the private sector, bank loans to the public sector, and overseas loans to the public sector. Loans from individuals or companies to the government (or vice versa) do not count as increasing the money supply, since the lender's spending power is reduced by the same amount as the borrower's gain in spending power.

So there has been a conscious policy in recent years not only to reduce the PSBR but also to reduce the proportion of it financed by borrowing from banks. Thus National Savings have been used to finance an increasingly large share of the PSBR. Treasury bills – which amount to a form of bank lending – have been steadily reduced and the main funding now comes overwhelmingly from the sale of gilts – 80 per cent of which are bought by non-bank institutions.

This objective has been so important to successive governments that in the words of the Treasury: 'largely as a consequence of the need to constrain monetary growth, debt sales to the non-bank private sector have in some years such 1977–78 and 1978–79 actually been greater than borrowing needs'. Governments actually *increase* their total borrowing in order to pursue monetary constraints without affecting the private sector.

The same theme recurs in other details of government borrowing. The increase in the proportion financed by national savings also reduces the need to sell gilts, which means that the demand for money in the City falls, thus 'allowing long-term interest rates to be lower than they would otherwise be' (to quote the Treasury again). Most starkly, the peculiar fact that the Bank of England actually lent over £2 billion to companies in 1980–81 and £4 billion in 1981–82, has a similar explanation. Short-term interest rates are now most influenced by the buying and selling of commercial bills issued by companies. In order to keep these interest rates lower than they would otherwise be, the Bank has actually been buying massive quantities of these commercial bills and has thus become a major lender to companies. The Treasury commented coolly that 'the effect of this was to add to the finance to be raised by other means'. Another way of putting it would be that all the money raised by national savings in these two years was used to finance private companies. The Tory government channelled far more public finance into industry in those two years than the National Enterprise Board was allowed under the Labour government. In early 1982 City commentators were actually welcoming this expansion of the Bank of England's lending to companies, as being an entirely legitimate reason for increasing public borrowing. Government borrowing is not treated as a problem if it is done for the benefit of business. The fundamental concern is thus clearly not with the money supply as such, but with reducing borrowing to finance public spending.

The other major consideration which influences the structure and level of government borrowing is the exchange rate. This factor is reflected in recent policies of reducing the amount of borrowing from overseas as a way of reducing the vulnerability of the pound. Thus in 1977–78 the government repaid £5,300 million of overseas debt – as much as the whole PSBR in that year. That year was a particularly significant illustration of how borrowing policy is influenced by financial considerations other than the PSBR itself, as it was the first year affected by the round of cuts in 1976, and a year when public spending was actually £4,000 million below the level planned after making cuts, because of the cash limits system. Yet the government actually borrowed more than enough money in Britain to finance the *original* level of spending plans, simply in order to reduce overseas indebtedness. For this purpose, a high level of borrowing was acceptable to the City – just as in 1981 it was acceptable to use a high level of borrowing to finance companies.

The government's overseas borrowing operations, as the Treasury put it, 'depend to a large extent on the authorities' stance on the exchange rate and conditions in the foreign exchange markets . . . changes in the reserves are an important source of of variation in the overseas sector's contribution'. The reserves are a fund held by the Bank of England to support the pound, and consist mainly of foreign currency. The exchange rate is fixed by the balance of supply and demand for the pound. When the Bank wants to support the pound, it buys sterling with the money in the reserves, and when it wants the pound to go down, it sells sterling. So building up the reserves is a way of strengthening the government's control over the value of the pound. In 1977, the reserves were massively increased, as a response to the sterling crises of the previous year. Foreign currency was bought, thus in effect reducing overseas debt, and hence the government in 1977–78 borrowed as much just to build up the reserves as it did to finance the PSBR.

These policies continued under the Tories. Between 1978 and early 1981 the value of the reserves, conventionally measured in US dollars, increased from $15,000 million to $28,000 million. In 1975 they had been worth only $5,400 million.

By October 1981 the reserves were much higher than the total of foreign currency debts. *The Financial Times* commented that 'since foreign interest income is now presumably greater than payments to service outstanding foreign currency loans, there is a chance that Britain may make a profit on official foreign exchange transactions'.

Thus operations to control the exchange rate have been a major factor in the government's borrowing programme over recent years. The way this has been done has been in effect to make the Bank of England a big and profitable dealer in the currency markets, thus injecting confidence into those markets (whose major dealers are now multinational companies). The cost has been high. The reduction in overseas currency liabilities between May 1979 and October 1980 accounted for about one-sixth of all the public sector borrowing during that period, and almost as much as the total cuts in public spending made in the first two years of the Tory government. The same level of government borrowing could have financed public spending programmes at the same level planned before the Tories made cuts, had there not been this deliberate policy of reducing foreign currency debt. The cuts were, in effect, used to restore the confidence of the financial markets – as they had been in 1976.

Summary

This account of the borrowing process highlights a number of points. First, government borrowing is not a costly extravagance financing profligate spending, but a normal financial activity which carries little or no real cost. Second, government financial operations are not simply a matter of finding the money for spending, but of transactions designed to achieve other objectives in line with the wishes of the markets. Third, the markets object only to government borrowing to finance public spending – borrowing to reduce bank credit, to build up reserves, or to finance industry is acceptable. Table 6 summarises the various purposes of government borrowing (see p. 111).

The key problem is not the technical niceties of economic theory, or the 'correct' level of the PSBR. It is that the interests of finance can and do make effective political demands against the interests of public service workers and communities. The borrowing arrangements allow these political pressures free rein.

This political power is perhaps the starkest problem faced by socialists. It is important to recognise it as a political problem, not a technical economic matter. The value of public services on the one hand is confronted by the values of financial capital on the other.

5.

Control Centre

While one part of the Treasury is busy oiling the wheels of the City, another part keeps patiently turning the cycles of public spending plans and controls. The latter may be less glamorous work – nevertheless, the City would be the first to acknowledge its importance.

These planning and control systems are as politically loaded as the aspects looked at so far. They ensure that the concerns of 'taxpayers' and financiers get priority over demands for public services. They are operated in secret, away from dangerous public debate about the politics of the decisions. The planning cycle, the cash limits system, and other key devices are even put subtly beyond the reach of parliamentary pressures for improved services. This chapter looks at just how undemocratic, unpublic, and politically biased, these supposedly innocuous systems are.

Secret planning

Public spending plans are drawn up annually in a cycle that stretches over the full twelve months of each financial year. This system was set up in the 1960s. Before then spending decisions could be made on an ad hoc basis, with no forward planning, and without any central co-ordination under the Treasury. The new system introduced the idea that all spending plans be brought together by Treasury officials, within the framework of overall Treasury economic plans, in consultation with top departmental officials. The committee of civil servants which brings all these top officials together is the Public Expenditure Survey Committee, from which the shorthand name of PESC comes.

The PESC cycle centres around the Treasury, starting with guidelines which they issue to departments, continuing with Treasury co-ordination of departmental plans, and the Treasury submission of proposals to cabinet within the framework of a Treasury analysis of economic prospects and the needs of industry, through ministerial appeals to Treasury ministers, to the final announcement of government decisions by the Chancellor of the Exchequer.

The cycle starts when the Treasury issues guidelines which tell government departments the basis on which they must start preparing their proposals for the first year covered by the plans. This is over twelve months before the start of the financial year in question. In January 1976, for example, they required departments to keep within existing total plans for the year 1977–78, to find compensating savings for any proposed increases in parts of these total plans, and additionally to identify further cuts of 5 per cent. Under the new cash planning arrangements (see below) the Treasury also lays down what assumptions to use about pay and price rises for future years. In December 1981, departments were told to assume 6 per cent price rises during 1983–84.

These initial guidelines obviously place considerable restraints on the scope for later decisions. Both the possible variations from previous plans and the price levels to be assumed are fixed, and are politically difficult to alter at later stages. The guidelines are usually secret, and issued to departmental officials by Treasury officials on the authority of the Chancellor of the Exchequer; they are not based on any public consultation or discussions. This pattern characterises the whole system. Political decisions, with serious implications for public services, are fed into the machine without the opportunity for public argument about the implications.

In the next stage, officials of the various government departments are responsible for putting together their 'bids' to the Treasury, within the guidelines laid down. Within each department, finance officials push their colleagues to suggest savings for any proposed increases. If primary schools want more resources, then technical colleges may be asked to make compensating cuts. Finance officials carry on discussions with the Treasury during this period, and these feed back into the internal departmental discussions. Ministers get involved only rarely, when officials believe it is necessary.

This whole process of 'divide and rule' sorts out who gets what at whose expense, and involves administrators in playing fascinating games and ploys to try and put one over on other administrators. A whole literature has sprung up for those who find such games the very essence of public administration. In practice this is how the idea that public spending problems are a matter of priorities gets applied – in secret, within the Treasury guidelines on available finance and largely by senior government officials. Finance rules, and services are made to squabble over shares. It is not permissible for NHS officials to suggest that their needs could be met by increasing taxes on the rich or multinationals.

Outsiders are only involved in a consultative capacity. In departments responsible for spending which is carried out by local authorities, there are working parties between the policy divisions of the relevant departments and representatives of the various local authority associations. The local authority associations that deal with the various government departments are separate and do not always have any common line; moreover, their role is only consultative, and they do not have any direct discussions with the Treasury. Councils thus have to rely on getting representatives from their associations to influence departmental officials to argue some kind of case for them to Treasury officials for later submission to the cabinet.

There are no other formal consultations at this stage. Notably, there is no joint working party between the DHSS and health authorities or the DES and the University Grants Committee.

As a result of these discussions, a series of spending projections which have been negotiated between the department and the Treasury is put together and formally agreed by the PESC committee itself. This Treasury-drafted report is then submitted to the cabinet in July by the Chancellor of Exchequer, as part of the 'Red Book', which is secret. This sets out the projected plans for the next three years for the different services, and for general items like a contingency reserve, debt interest and sales of nationalised industry assets to arrive at the overall total expenditure envisaged.

Alongside this material is an economic assessment from the Treasury of how much room is left for public expenditure in the coming years in the light of its economic forecast and views on the needs of business (and, under the cash planning system, pay and price assumptions for the coming years).

In the July 1977 Red Book the Treasury stated that there was overall scope for increasing public spending in future years – but that since they wished to increase the contingency reserve (of which more later) by an amount larger than the available increase, the actual programmes would have to be cut!

The first relevant cabinet meeting takes place in July (this is why there are invariably reports of an 'emergency' or 'crisis' meeting on the economy in July). Sometimes, there may be an initial package of decisions agreed and announced at once, if the external situation is felt to require it, as happened in 1976. More usually, the broad outlines of the approach to plans are agreed, and decisions on detail are sorted out over a period of months through a series of meetings between ministers and Treasury ministers, known as bi-laterals. In 1981, these discussions were conducted through two cabinet committees, the second of which was chaired by the Prime Minister.

One key decision that now has to be taken by September (previously it was not necessary until December) is the specific pay and price rise assumptions for the coming year. This sets the limit on the cash allowed for public service pay rises, and also indicates the extent to which inflation is to be allowed to erode public spending by fixing the limit allowed for the rise in the price of other inputs purchased by the public sector. The provisional overall figure set in the previous September is likely to be maintained, but may be distributed differently between pay and price rises. For instance, in September 1981 the government decided that pay would be assumed to rise by 4 per cent in 1982–83, and other prices by 9 per cent. The net result, after allowing for the importance of pay in public spending, was the same as the assumption of 7 per cent overall pay and price rises in 1982–83 which had been fixed in September 1980. This decision may be weighted by considerations other than the Treasury's assessment. In 1980, the Treasury was prepared to allow a rise of 8 per cent or 9 per cent in public service pay in 1981–82, but the cabinet, influenced by the pay offer made by BL cars that week, decided to impose 6 per cent as the limit.

Final decisions on programmes are usually reached by December, when the plans are now generally announced. The Rate Support Grant is announced in the same month.

The plans are further refined after the December decisions, by departmental officials working out precisely how the total sums given to each programme will be allocated to the various parts of the programmes. Thus the cabinet decisions are akin to awarding lump sums to each department, which then has the freedom of allocation (although the Treasury checks the final breakdown).

Until final decisions have been made, there is no information published, no parliamentary debate, and no opportunity to exercise political pressures on decisions for anyone other than top officials, ministers, and those who are granted political access to them. The public services simply wait and rely on any sympathy, commitment and diplomatic skills that the select band of participants may deploy. The only source of public information is leaks to the press – which are more often stage-managed by the Treasury than the result of investigative brilliance.

Cash limits rule

The cycle described above is the way that plans are made for spending on public services. Once the spending actually starts, there are further systems for controlling what is spent. These were developed in the mid-1970s by the Labour government to deal with two problems. First, after plans had been set, it was possible to mount political pressure during the year to increase the resources for a service – for example, education – above the planned allocation, without any offsetting savings. Second, money used to be automatically added to public service budgets to take account of inflation. As prices rose, or a pay settlement was reached, extra money was supplied to maintain real resources at planned levels.

The first problem was dealt with by an obscure but crucial administrative ploy. Public spending plans had always included a figure, the contingency reserve, as an estimate of possible later additions. In 1975, the Treasury persuaded the Labour cabinet to change its role dramatically. Ministerial standing orders were amended to state that in future the contingency reserve would be an absolute ceiling on any subsequent cabinet decisions on public spending. Ever since, that innocuous-looking figure has been a predetermined constraint on the political freedom, even of ministers, to increase spending as a whole. The rules of the cabinet itself now enshrine the priority of financial considerations over the requirements of public services.

The second problem was dealt with by the introduction of the cash limits system. It is cash limits that now function as the overriding determinant of the amount of actual spending governments are prepared to finance. Other figures of plans, targets, etc., are of peripheral importance in controlling what is spent. The system was introduced by the Wilson government in 1975, for the financial year 1976–77, and has not been substantially changed since.

They are, as their name implies, sums of money which are set before the start of a financial year to indicate the maximum amount of cash that the government is prepared to spend. All central government spending, except for social security payments and one or two minor items, are subject to cash limits. There is a cash limit for the Department of Energy's spending, another for the Manpower Services Commission, and so on . . . The whole of the NHS has one cash limit, which is distributed among health authorities by the DHSS. Local government capital spending is now governed by cash limits on expenditure, and the Rate Support Grant to councils for current spending is subject to a cash limit. The only major element of public spending on services not subject to cash limits is the amount of council spending financed by rates – which goes some way to explaining the Tories' attempts to control the total of council spending by various other tortuous devices, discussed in the next chapter.

Because cash limits are set before the start of the financial year to which they relate, they depend on prefixed assumptions about the rise in pay and prices. (This was as true under the old system of planning using constant prices as it is now under the 'cash' planning system: the only difference is that the assumptions now have to fixed a couple of months earlier.) It is these assumptions that effectively set an incomes policy for public service pay. They also effectively fix what can be spent on services.

The principle of the control exercised through cash limits is a simple one. Whatever the actual rise in prices, whatever the actual need for services and workers to provide them, no more money will be forthcoming. The political conflicts between the real level of services and public sector pay, on the one hand, and the amount of finance available from taxation or borrowing, on the other, are thus automatically resolved in favour of finance: the workers and the public have to fit in as best they can.

Cash limits are fixed on the basis of a cabinet decision, and can only be altered by a cabinet decision. Since 1979, they have been submitted for formal approval by parliament; this development presents a further obstacle to their being altered, since changes now require not only a cabinet decision but a parliamentary vote as well.

There are three common misunderstandings about cash limits. First, it is sometimes suggested that the cash limits system could be made flexible, so that the limits are revised upwards if prices rise more than assumed. It is indeed technically possible to increase the financial provision for services in line with actual inflation – this was exactly what happened normally before the introduction of cash limits. But to return to operating in such a way would be to destroy the point of the system. As Leo Pliatsky, the Treasury official who master-minded the introduction of cash limits, has observed: 'If it were believed that they [cash limits] could be exceeded with impun-ity, in the expectation of a higher cash limit, we should be no better off and there would be no point in the new system.'

The new system *has* worked. Revisions of cash limits have been very rare (apart from minor and technical adjustments) and have all occurred under the Tory government – contrary to some implicit assertions that Labour was less rigid. The first major Tory revision took place after the May 1979 election, because the strikes of 1978–79 had achieved pay settlements which could not possibly be contained within the limits inher-ited from Labour. The other major revisions have been made to allow the defence budget to breach its cash limit, which reflects the overriding political priority given by the Tories to their commitment to increasing the real level of defence provi-sion.

A second misrepresentation, popular with establishment academics and 'moderate' politicians, is the suggestion that cash limits are a method of 'monitoring' public spending. This is like suggesting that income tax is a way of monitoring people's income. Cash limits don't monitor *anything*, they just limit spending. An excellent monitoring system – the Treas-ury's Financial Information System (FIS) – has in fact been introduced to improve the enforcement of cash limits. This could operate perfectly well without any cash limits being set. FIS monitors, cash limits limit.

The third, related, misrepresentation is popular with the Labour establishment. It is the suggestion that it is only under the Tories that cash limits have been used as an incomes policy. However, the original political purpose of cash limits is a matter of historical record. Denis Healey's April 1975 budget statement referred to pay settlements in the public services prompting a serious consideration of cash limits, and he announced the new system on 1 July 1975 with the words: 'We propose to fix cash limits for wage bills in the public sector' and later: 'I propose to employ the system of cash limits more generally as a means of controlling public expenditure in the short term.' The first objective was to curb public service pay, and the second was to override political pressures for maintaining or increasing the real value of public spending. The Tories have always been prepared to give Labour full credit for these innovations.

Cash limits have worked. That is, they have consistently forced cuts in services below 'planned' levels. One reason is the consistent and deliberate underestimates of inflation built into the limits, so that even spending the full cash amount has meant real cuts in the level of services. Another is that the Treasury has ruled that breach of cash limits will be treated as 'financial maladministration', thus terrorising administrators who fear the budgetary and personal consequences of running out of money before the end of the year. As a result, spending usually does not even reach the full amount allowed by the cash limits.

The setting of cash limits is now probably the most important art of public administration. The simplest part is to decide how much to allow for pay and price rises in the coming year, and the usual approach is to take the expected rate of price rises generally and require public service prices to rise by less than that. So for 1981–82 it was assumed that public pay and prices would rise by 9 per cent, compared with general prices expected to rise by 11 per cent. This meant, very simply, that the public services would be eroded by forcing them to absorb 2 per cent of inflation. In fact, inflation was nearer 12 per cent, implying a real cut of nearly 3 per cent. And administrators did not spend the full amount: non-defence cash limits were underspent by 3.3 per cent. The total cuts delivered by the system thus came to 6.3 per cent. Table 2 shows the effects since 1976–77 (see p. 108).

This administrative squeeze erodes services, jobs and conditions without any open political decision to do so: it all takes place automatically as the result of innumerable decisions of managers under pressure. Ministers have the enviable position of requiring cuts without having to take responsibility for the specific cuts that result. The administrative squeeze is both effective and invisible except to those affected, and even they can never know that it was the cash limit from ministers which caused their loss of job or service.

Further refinements are possible within the system. There is the trick of requiring extra work or extra payments but not increasing the cash limits to cover them. An early example was when the Labour government required public authorities to implement the Health and Safety at Work Act for their employees, but did not give them the extra £10 million needed to do this – the cash limits remained unchanged. So health and safety could only be implemented by cuts and squeezes elsewhere. A more vicious refinement is when cash limits are not increased to allow for extra taxes that public bodies have to pay into the government's own funds. Thus in 1979, when VAT shot up, the NHS faced extra costs of £40 million because of the price rises that followed. So health services and jobs had to be cut just to pay over VAT from the government to the government! The approach reached new heights in the 1982 budget, which reduced employers' National Insurance contributions but increased fuel tax. The first reduced the costs of public bodies, the second increased them. Cash limits were adjusted *down* to take account of the drop in National Insurance, but not *up* to allow for the increased fuel costs.

Incredible as it may sound, another technique in setting the cash limits is to take away the number you first thought of. Even after deciding on the pay and price assumptions, the Treasury normally knocks off an arbitrary percentage before reaching the final figure. Thus the limits for 1982–83 were calculated after allowing for pay rises of 4 per cent, price rises of 9 per cent and then knocking 2 per cent off everything. This is sometimes called efficiency, or good housekeeping: the Labour government tended to do this at an earlier stage in the calculations, by reducing basic plans by 1 per cent or 2 per cent for luck.

The cash limits system is one of the most important parts of the whole cuts machine. It manages to fulfil the political roles of giving priority to finance, discounting the value of services, disciplining workers, and limiting the opportunity for contrary influences. The effect on workers is discussed in Chapter 7.

Funny money

A more recent innovation is the system of 'cash planning'. This is often confused with cash limits, but is a different, separate and later development. It relates to the price basis used in calculating the figures in spending plans.

Since 1981, the government has changed all public spending planning from the old 'volume' basis to a new 'cash' basis. The volume basis used figures calculated so as to ignore the effect of changes in pay levels and in the prices of other resources on which the money was spent. Thus the figures for all past years' spending, and all plans for forthcoming years, were expressed in terms of the prices at a single date. For example, if a programme required employing 100 clerical workers whose pay was £5,000 per year in 1980–81, then that programme would be set down as costing £500,000 per year not only in 1980–81, but also in 1979–80, 1981–82 and every other year in which the same number of workers were employed on that pay scale. So any changes from one year to another in the programmes meant that there was a change in the number of people employed or the amount of goods purchased. Although there were many problems with this method (see Chapter 2 above), the figures were conventionally regarded as a proxy for the level of services to be provided, and it was possible to see how the actual spending during a year matched with the planned level, or how spending plans for one year compared with the spending on resources in previous years, or how the new plans for a year compared with earlier plans for that year.

In 1981, however, the government stopped using this system altogether. Now they do not even calculate spending in volume terms for internal purposes. Instead, plans are drawn up simply in terms of the amount of cash which the government intends to allow to be spent (and past years are also recorded simply in terms of the cash spent, with no adjustment for inflation). These kinds of plans were urged by a number of monetarists, who used to jibe that the old 'volume' plans were based on 'funny money'.

But the new system uses the funniest money of all – using

various price levels which have never existed and are not
expected to exist in the future. Thus the 1982 White Paper
presented the expected outturn for 1981–82 on the basis of the
price and pay levels it had forecast during 1980 – which were
known to be definitely wrong by 1982! And its plans for
1982–83 were even 'funnier', being based on the fictional
1981–82 prices uprated by further assumptions for 1982–83
which were generally expected to be equally fictional. Ironically, at the same time as public spending plans were being put
onto this fantasy basis, there were now new proposals published for companies to stop presenting their profit record in
terms of cash – which *The Financial Times* described as 'per-
petuating the illusion of inflation-fuelled growth' – and instead
to adjust previous years' performance into the prices of the
current year, which the *FT* welcomed as a 'brave' new practice.
This brave new method was of course how public spending
used to be presented, until the change to the cash system with
its built-in illusion of inflation-fuelled growth.

This illusion is in fact one of the main points of the new
planning basis. When inflation is running at 10 per cent, the
government can claim that anything spent which is greater than
a 10 per cent cut on the previous year's volume is an increase,
and the information to challenge this is not available. It is no
longer possible to see what volume cuts are planned, or how
the previous year's outturn compared with the plans for that
year. The obscurity and lack of information in cash plans are
their key feature. They abandon any pretence to value public
services, and simply treat them as consumers of so much money
which is grudgingly allocated in large lumps. The only connec-
tion with services now lies in the allocation of money to one
government department rather than another.

Parliamentary inaction

So far, parliament has hardly been mentioned in this chapter.
The reason is that the role of parliament in the planning and
control systems is extremely limited. It is especially difficult for
it to restrain cuts. MPs are not allowed to propose increases in

public spending. There is a standing order of the House of Commons, dating from the early eighteenth century, which forbids anyone other than a government minister from putting forward motions for spending public money. This was strengthened in 1866 to close some loopholes, and a wide-ranging report from a Select Committee in 1981, which was concerned precisely with the powers of parliament over public spending, concluded that the convention should remain. Erskine May, the 'bible' of parliamentary procedure, regards the issue as important enough to merit several pages explaining that the practice is far more fundamental to the constitution than even its status as a standing order, and spends some further pages affirming that a few apparent precedents for minor relaxation of the rule should certainly not be followed now. Technically, votes on public spending proposals are treated as though they concerned gifts to the royal family.

So only the government can propose plans for spending. These cannot be amended upwards by MPs, either as individuals or as the opposition: they can only be accepted or rejected *in toto*. Thus MPs are not allowed to move that services be improved, or that public service workers should be given more pay: the constitutional principle insists that the issue is always and only public spending.

The only part of the whole planning system which requires parliamentary decisions is approval of the Supply Estimates. These cover most public spending, except that which comes out of National Insurance contributions or the rates. The passing of the Estimates has invariably been done without even debating the matters to which the Estimates relate. The time is instead used for debates on subjects chosen by the opposition, and concludes with a formal vote approving the supply of money in the Estimates. Although they can in theory be rejected, they never are in practice. Recent reforms will make a slight difference to the amount of debate, however.

The planning process described earlier, which leads up to the formulation of the Estimates, does not involve parliament at all. The PESC planning cycle is conducted entirely by civil servants and ministers, in secret. The only comprehensive statement of government spending plans, the annual White Paper on Public Expenditure, is a purely consultative document which does not need approval from parliament. The White Papers submitted by the Labour government in 1976 and 1977 were actually rejected by the House of Commons. On both occasions, a vote of confidence followed, which the government won: the original spending plans were then implemented regardless of the result of the vote on them. Joel Barnett, then Chief Secretary to the Treasury, treats these experiences with amused indifference in his memoirs.

Thus parliamentary authority is not required to make *cuts* in spending. Just as the White Paper cuts were implemented with blithe disregard for parliamentary votes, so too, before 1979, were cash limits – they were set by government as a purely administrative exercise, and never even debated. They are now incorporated in the Estimates, and thus subject to the same rule that MPs cannot even propose that they be increased!

Summary

These procedures are at the heart of the cuts machine. The process of government itself is part of the undemocratic and loaded pressures against public services. If parliamentary democracy cannot even provide for democratic politics to influence the public services, it is not surprising that there is widespread disillusion with Westminster. Nor is it surprising that ministerial acceptance of responsibility for providing services is becoming obsolete. The process is neither open nor responsive to the needs of people.

6.

Auxiliary Controls

If cash limits are the key engine of the cuts machine, they have a number of auxiliaries supporting them in their work. The majesty of the law is not a politically neutral observer of the public services, but plays a part in curbing them. The grey profession of auditors has also played a significant role over the years. And there are a number of subsidiary systems for putting pressure on public services. This chapter looks at the ones squeezing local councils and the NHS.

Lawyers and auditors

Judges have been a boon to an establishment concerned not only with trade union organisation but also with political swings to the left in local democracy. Cases in 1982 focused on the transport policies of the GLC and other authorities, but the origins of these cases and the House of Lords judgement in the GLC case pose wider threats to council services and workers.

The year 1981 saw a spate of cases initiated against rate increases, largely by companies. In the West Midlands, BL Cars brought proceedings against 'unreasonable' rate rises; in London, cases were initiated by Bromley Council, Westminster Chamber of Commerce, and a small group of Camden ratepayers. Aims of Industry also mounted a £200,000 campaign against the GLC, backed by a number of large companies.

The House of Lords upheld the Bromley case against the GLC, thus forcing the council to abandon a policy on which it had been elected. Their ruling was not even restricted to transport. It re-emphasised the priority of councils' 'fiduciary responsibility to ratepayers', a recurrent theme of court rulings on local government over the years. Lord Denning, in the Appeal Court, had also suggested that the party manifesto on which a council election was won was not something councillors should feel bound to follow.

This decision led to the West Midlands County Council dropping its cheap fares policy. And, in July 1982, the Secretary of State for Transport referred to the threat of court cases as one way in which government policies could be enforced on recalcitrant councils. Not all cases have resulted in legal defeats for councils. Merseyside won a judgement in favour of its transport policy. One case against Camden Council also failed – fortunately, since the ratepayers' grouping wanted among other things a ruling that a council 'is not entitled to pursue political objectives regardless of the ratepayers' expense'. There were also technical victories in the rulings that the government acted illegally in suspending Southwark Area Health Authority, and in super-penalising London councils for overspending. The first decision was, however, reversed by legislation, and the second merely insisted on 'prior consultation' – the penalties were still imposed.

Legislation has also been used by the Tory government to restructure the controls on public services. Apart from the specific legislation on local government finance, a spate of Acts in 1980 shifted the balance further away from services and towards spending restraints. Various duties to provide services were lifted, including the duty to provide nursery education, and the duty to build council housing to a given standard. At the same time new duties were imposed, including ones requiring health authorities to keep within cash limits at whatever cost to health care, and councils to offer council houses for sale.

The general impact of much of this legislation has been to emphasise duties of financial trusteeship and minimise the duties to provide services. It is increasingly a matter of political indifference what services are being provided, or whether they are provided, so long as the budget is not exceeded. When Enfield Health Authority stopped all admissions of psycho-geriatric patients, the DHSS took the view that their duty to provide such a service was not absolute: 'other local priorities and financial resources may legitimately place constraints upon the provision of particular facilities'.

Local government auditors have long been important in imposing cuts and curtailing council democracy. Although their job appeared to be merely to examine council accounts for 'unlawful' expenditure, court rulings have made it clear that their function relates primarily to minimising rates and spending. In the House of Lords judgement on Poplar Council delivered in the 1920s, Lord Sumner declared:'The purpose of the statutory audit . . . is the protection of the ratepayers' pockets and not the immunity of spendthrift administration.'

While headline cases like Poplar and Clay Cross are rare, the years from 1979 saw a spate of activity by auditors against the policies of Labour councils. Camden council was denounced in an auditors' report for paying more than the final national settlement in the 1979 manual workers' dispute, and this political judgement was enforced by the threat of surcharge. Less directly, the expectation of disapproval by the auditor was a real factor in decisions by Lothian Council and the Inner London Education Authority to change their policies. The auditor of Brent Council actually gave an advance policy hint in 1981, observing that an increase in rents 'seems to me to be unavoidable'. By contrast, auditors' reports on undervaluation of council houses for sale have either been followed by no threat of legal action (as in Westminster Council) or have effectively ruled that the political principle of council house sales is greater than the principle of tight financing (as in Nottingham).

The recognition of the political potential of auditing the public sector has produced a number of strands of pressure. First, there has been direct encouragement to council auditors to engage in 'value-for-money' auditing (VFM). Indeed this is a duty of auditors under the 1982 Local Government Finance Act. An auditor is now statutorily obliged to 'satisfy himself' that a council 'has made proper arrangements for securing economy, efficiency and effectiveness in its use of resources'. The new Audit Commission is obliged to make studies on the impact of statutory duties or ministerial guidelines 'on economy, effectiveness and efficiency in the provision of local authority services'.

All this means that auditors, and the Commission, will have far more scope for pronouncing on such matters as staffing levels, bonus schemes, the use of direct labour, and even on the level of rents and charges. This approach fits in with the ideas of judges about the 'problem' of local authority extravagance, and with the pressure from the CBI and other business interests to force councils to be more 'businesslike' and make more cuts. The Association of Certified Accountants, the largest international accountancy body in the world, told Michael Heseltine that it was 'gravely concerned at the dangers of the auditor's proper role, function and responsibilites being confused with . . . the pressures on him, from others than those to whom his duty lies, for work which is more properly seen as management consultancy than as auditing'. Given political conflicts between central and local government, they said that 'we cannot see how an auditor can readily avoid appearing . . . as less than objective and independent in his comments on the relative merits of these competitive objectives'. Even the auditors' own representatives fear that the new law makes their job too obviously political.

Second, the government has encouraged, and in some cases required the use of private accountants to audit and scrutinise council operations. Fourteen councils were ordered – under a dubious interpretation of the 1972 Act – to appoint private accountants in 1981. Other special private surveys have been commissioned, with predictable results. One, by Coopers and Lybrand, looked at 26 councils and recommended contracting out more work. Another, by a team of businesspeople called in by Peterborough City Council, called for a reduction in operating levels and for hiving off of services to the private sector. Auditors have been enjoying a bonanza in council work.

Third, the Monopolies Commission is now being used systematically, under the 1980 Competition Act, to investigate the efficiency of nationalised industries and water boards.

Fourth, the House of Commons Public Accounts Committee

(PAC), supported by accountancy bodies, has argued for a comprehensive audit office for the whole of the public sector, based on the present office of the Comptroller and Auditor General. This office would be under the control of parliament and not the government. This approach has been opposed by the Tory government. Although it has the institutional merit of independence from government, such a proposal shares the objectives of strengthening audit to examine VFM, and acting as a watchdog on the excesses of public bodies. Parliamentary committees do not have an outstanding record for the jobs, pay and working conditions of public employees, and recent investigations by these committees confirm that audit is seen simply as another channel for extracting greater 'efficiency'.

Fifth, the PAC has already started making greater use of their audits in central government to apply VFM and other pressures on workers and services. Similar use is now also being made of audit in the NHS.

Controlling councils

The use of government controls over local authority spending since 1976 has been based on indifference to services coupled with strict requirements of financial stewardship. Most of the key innovations stem from the Local Government, Planning and Land Act 1980, and the new Local Government Finance Act 1982. These novel forms of control are distinct from more traditional methods such as reducing the level of support provided through the Rate Support Grant (RSG), or political bias in the distribution of RSG – both techniques have been used by recent Labour and Tory administrations alike.

The most prominent of these new controls is the new method for calculating a council's government grant. Under the previous RSG system, the 'needs' element of the RSG was calculated by reference to councils' actual spending on services, which was in effect treated as a proxy for social needs. The new block grant system is based on 'grant related expenditure' – which is a centrally calculated assessment of what local authorities *should* be spending to provide comparable services. Since this bears little or no relation to what services and spending councils actually undertake, the basis for grant distribution is shifted significantly from any notion of supporting services.

The new system is also based on assumptions about the level of rates levied by councils, and effectively requires a much higher proportion of spending above government-approved levels to be financed out of rates – or preferably, from the government's point of view, to be cut. A complex series of measures are now in operation to enforce this policy by curtailing the grant available to 'high-spending' authorities. The net effect is to reduce the influence of local political decisions about services on the finance provided, which is now more dependent on central government decisions about proper financing levels and local 'ratepayers' agitation'.

The statutory position in Scotland is even starker, since the Scottish Office has powers to reduce its grant to authorities which are deemed to be spending unreasonably, and require either cuts or rate reductions to be made to obtain the grant. The case of Lothian Council in 1981 showed the use of these powers.

As has been frequently pointed out, the new powers under the 1980 and 1982 Acts represent an increase in central controls over local authorities. But they are controls based on central stewardship of finance, rather than explicit decisions on particular local policies. Lothian was left free in 1981 to make the cuts where it liked. It is a repeated theme of the Tory government that distribution of cuts is left to local authorities themselves, whether these are required as a result of curtailed spending plans in the White Paper, cash limits, cuts in the level of the Rate Support Grant or the array of penalties under the new block grant.

The sharpest recent example of this principle, in another area, was the university cuts of 1981, when the UGC was given the task of distributing the cuts entirely as it pleased. The government could remain distant from any political involvement in the consequences; even when the lecturers' union indicated a readiness to discuss pay adjustments as an input to the process, Keith Joseph could simply refer them to the UGC as the proper body with whom to work out such matters. There are now plans to control local authority higher education through a similar mechanism.

The growth of central government control over, and pressures on, council spending on services, has strengthened support for restructuring local government finance to give more control over taxation to councils themselves. However, as President Reagan's initiative to devolve a number of major services from the federal budget to the state level has demonstrated, maximum devolution of revenue-raising and spending powers is not necessarily a progressive step. One of the options canvassed in 1982, following a government Green Paper on rates, would in fact have got close to that position for many services: that was the idea that education should become completely centrally financed, as is the health service, and that councils would then finance locally all the other services that they wish to provide, with minimum central support. Such devolution favours rich areas, where money can be raised more easily with low tax rates, and deters any councils from providing higher levels of service than others do – ratepaying businesses emigrate, and people with high needs for services move in.

Local authorities obtain their money from a variety of sources: rates, which are paid by local residents to the council; rents paid by council tenants; charges for such services as fares and school meals; sale of property such as council houses; borrowing; grants from central government (which in turn are raised by taxes and borrowing); and other minor sources such as lotteries and EEC grants. Although rates were originally the major source of income, government grants are now the biggest provider of money – and tenants and local users of services pay nearly as much as the total amount raised on the rates.

The distribution of this financing burden is a political issue. Some Labour councils deliberately try to reduce the burden on local people by holding down fares or rents. Companies try to reduce the amount of rates they pay by using the courts or the media. Recent governments have tried to make councils raise more money through higher rents and charges, selling council houses, and even running lotteries. And they have forced local people to pay a bigger share by reducing government grants.

Squeezes on councils in the 1970s led to charges being increased. Since 1979 the Tory government has increased the pressure by forcing rent rises and assuming higher charges for a range of services. An extreme example of the effects of this pressure is East Cambridgeshire. By 1982 this council had raised rents so high that it was almost able to abolish rates.

Money against health

Sources of finance are even more obviously a political issue in the NHS. Here there are four sources of finance: taxation; National Insurance contributions; charges; and charity. All except charity are controlled by central government. Nearly 90 per cent of NHS income comes from taxation, and the amount going to the NHS is effectively determined through the public spending planning process.

National Insurance stamps have included for many years a specific amount for the health service. This originated before the NHS was set up, when there was a scheme of partial health insurance for some employees. This has never been a large proportion of NHS funding, and by 1981 produced less than 10 per cent of finance. It is, however, a politically sensitive area, since there are still strong pressures to replace the NHS in whole or in part with an insurance scheme under which entitlement to treatment would depend on contributions paid. In 1981 the Tory government examined the operation of such schemes in other countries, and the NHS portion of National Insurance contributions was raised in both 1981 and 1982.

Charges account for a small but growing proportion of health finance – currently around 3 per cent. Originally, all treatment under the NHS was free, but over the years successive governments have steadily increased charges for prescriptions, dental treatment and glasses. Such charges are not really financially significant to the NHS (in 1979–80 the underspend on health services was 1½ times the income from charges), but they inculcate the idea that the patient should pay for treatment. This political loading is reflected in the presentation of increased charges as reductions in NHS spending. If a budget stated that revenue was in future to be raised by taxing people for being sick, it might raise eyebrows. But that is what charges amount to.

The tradition of charity for local hospitals goes back a long way. Under the NHS, it has continued, with local people commonly making collections to help provide, for example, extra toys for a children's hospital. But until 1980 it was never regarded as a source of funds for the NHS itself, but simply as a bonus. Under the 1980 Health Act, however, the state's responsibility for funding the NHS was changed. Now, the state's finance is just 'towards meeting the expenditure', and health authorities are specifically empowered to raise money through jumble sales and the like. The threat is, again, to undermine the principle that health should be financed out of national resources. It also means that disproportionate finance may be raised for 'attractive' aspects of medicine, like expensive equipment, and less on already disadvantaged areas like geriatrics and mental illness. In 1979–80 charity provided £33 million to the NHS – about 0.4 per cent of total spending.

The politics of finance are fundamental to the health service. The notorious 1982 cabinet think-tank report recommended that health finance should be switched to private insurance, thus reducing public spending on health. The political bias inherent in this kind of accounting was discussed in Chapter 2. It is also linked with the systematic encouragement of private medicine which has occurred since 1979.

Yet private medicine's finances are never presented in full. It is parasitic on the NHS. It takes advantage of labour trained at NHS expense and operates in NHS hospitals where much labour is provided free. It also relies on the NHS to deal with all the unprofitable work and, crucially, to take as emergencies private patients who cannot be properly cared for in private hospitals. But the state is encouraging the expansion of the profitable private sector in a number of ways: by pressing health authorities to pay private hospitals to do contract work where the NHS is left with insufficient resources; by relaxing planning controls; and by encouraging private insurance.

The squeeze on the NHS has been intensified by the administration of controls over state finance. As in other public services, the basis of controls is the cash limits system. Since the 1980 Act, it has been a statutory requirement for health authorities to keep within their cash limits, even if this means failing to provide some of the services that they are supposedly obliged by law to operate. Some of the squeezes have been a deliberate result of fixing cash limits. In 1979–80 for example, the increase in VAT in the budget meant higher prices for the NHS, but the cash limit was not increased to allow for this, and so cuts had to be made just to pay the extra VAT to the government. The result was a 2.4 per cent cut in planned spending.

A further source of pressure has been the system of distributing money among health authorities, known as RAWP (after the 1975 Resource Allocation Working Party which devised the formulae). The laudable idea was to allocate funds more on the basis of need than did the previous system, under which prestigious teaching hospitals got a disproportionate amount of resources. So RAWP meant London lost money to other parts of the country, but, because the London regions cover areas of considerable deprivation as well as wealth, some poor areas have got an even worse deal from the NHS. A spate of hospital closures has occurred in unfashionable parts of London. Within regions, a similar process of allocation between districts is carried out, with cash limits being set by regional authorities for district authorities – all on the bigger fleas and lesser fleas principle.

There is one exception to these control systems. Family practitioner services – GPs – are not cash limited, nor are they directly managed by health authorities. They are instead given money according to demand (basically, patient registrations), and are then paid not as employees but as self-employed subcontractors. Moreover, the service is run by committees dominated by the GPs themselves. This unusual position originated in strike action by doctors in 1911, who refused to operate the then new health insurance scheme of Lloyd George, except on their own terms.

By 1982, the various pressures on finances were considerable. Numerous health authorities found themselves having to cut services to a point where their basic legal obligations were threatened. Outside London, regions found that they no longer had any 'growth money' coming from the redistributive effects of RAWP. The Oxford region released proposals for coping with their financial dilemma, which actually included the suggestion that new residents in the region would not be offered full services until they had lived in the area for a year.

Summary

The law, audit and the financial control systems all contribute to the squeeze on services. The methods of financing make a crucial political difference. None of this network can form part of socialist approaches, which need to be based on the values of services and not 'fiduciary' responsibility to financiers. Above all, they need to be based on the workers and users of the services.

7.

Squeezing the Workers

One of the main concerns of judges and auditors is the problem of the workers. It is a theme that runs through most public discussion of the 'problem' of public spending. The view of the Tory government, its Labour predecessor and the national press can be summarised as 'they're overpaid, over many, over protected and underproductive'.

A popular advocate of this view is retired civil servant Leslie Chapman. In his widely publicised book on how to make cuts, he wrote: 'I am writing about waste in the old fashioned sense – the waste involved in having ten men where five are enough.' Thus men (and presumably he includes women, too) are wasted by being *employed* and jobs are said to be 'saved' when they are destroyed.

Most components of the cuts machine focus on the workers. The accounting system regards their output as having no independent value and their productivity as unchanging. However much is squeezed out of workers in public services, for however little, there is always a basic presumption that they are too numerous, too well paid or too inefficient. The control systems of cash limits and the concern of auditors with value-for-money studies are both primarily concerned with reducing labour costs.

This chapter looks at some of the main ways in which governments have tried to squeeze public sector workers. Attacks on pay and conditions and stronger management controls are obvious parts of this attack and are familiar to all workers. More insidious has been the steady squeeze imposed by simply withdrawing staff and other resources from a service little by little. This has simultaneously put workers and services under pressure because the level of services resulting has been a matter of political indifference to governments. The only concern to maintain services has come from the users of services and the workers themselves.

Managing the servants

The public services are an increasingly important source of employment for people in Britain. In 1978 they employed over 5 million people, providing more than 20 per cent of all jobs in the country, having grown from just over 3 million people – 13 per cent of all jobs – in 1961. This growth was vital to the economy. Jobs in manufacturing fell by about 1,700,000 over the same period.

The structure of public service employment is characterised by using low-paid, often part-time female labour. The NHS is perhaps the classic example of this, where the largest group of workers – nurses – are overwhelmingly female, usually young, and are expected to do shiftwork both during and after training for pay which compares badly with that of unskilled male workers. Ancillary workers are also overwhelmingly female, often part-time, and are among the lowest paid workers in the country. And even the medical workers are structured so that junior doctors work exorbitant hours, and unpopular work like geriatrics is heavily dependent on foreign workers coming for the privilege of experience.

Local government and the civil service show a similar pattern, with a large proportion of low-paid women workers doing the bulk of clerical, typing, cleaning and catering work. Sixty per cent of local government manual workers are part-time women. Both the type of work they do and their designation as ancillaries or servants, reflect the traditional domestic role of women, whether working unpaid for their husbands or paid for the upper class or the state. And for similar reasons the plight of part-time women in such public service jobs receives a low priority from the traditional boiler-suited male core of the trade union movement. Even the greater sense of sympathy for nurses probably owes as much to traditional male protectiveness as it does to solidarity with fellow workers.

The employment of women is tied up with the lack of value ascribed to public services. The caring work of women in the home is not valued – or even paid – because it is not involved in profitable production. The caring work of the public services is largely done by women, who are not paid an 'industrial' wage because they are still not doing 'productive' work – and are not employed full-time because they are still expected to do unpaid domestic work as well. Exploitation of women's work and economic contempt for public services are two sides of the same coin.

The urge to cut the cost of public service workers has been intensified in recent years. There has been a drive to increase management controls and introduce business management techniques in all areas of the public services. This started in the 1960s , and one result was the reorganisation of management structures in local councils, the NHS, and the civil service. Another was the introduction of techniques such as work study into local government and the NHS, to help extract more output from fewer workers. Yet another has been the proliferation of special studies by consultants or accountants brought in from the model world of business – typified by the previously mentioned use of Sir Derek Rayner from Marks and Spencer to streamline the civil service.

The effect of all this has been the erosion of political control by councillors and ministers, reinforcing the trend noted in the previous chapter. The introduction of Chief Executives and corporate planning techniques in local government is one example of this. Another is the effect of cash limits in devolving authority to cut services to line management, without overt political decisions being taken. The degree of management control over previous work arrangements has also been strengthened. In the NHS, for example, the structures set up by Keith Joseph in 1974 gave much more authority to administrators than had existed previously, especially in relation to the medical profession. This was considerably enhanced by the introduction of cash limits, which were positively welcomed by NHS managers as giving them extra power and authority over the allocation of resources. In the civil service, the most striking results have been the series of Rayner reports, which have focused on reducing labour costs, enhancing the autonomy of line management, and reducing the public service claims on other resources. One report on the administration of social security offices recommended that staff should be hired and fired locally and employed on 5- or 11-month contracts; this would mean the elimination of any job protection rights which exist under civil service procedures and under the law on unfair dismissals.

Pay and conditions

Pay curbs matter to the government for a number of reasons. One is that pay is a large element in current public spending, and is identified in establishment discussions throughout the period as a key inflationary factor, pushing up the costs to 'the country' with no profitable return. Another is the general desire to contribute to the disciplining of labour and the depression of living standards in a period of economic crisis. As one academic observed, the principle of the government setting an example of good practice for other employees took on a new meaning in this period.

The main attack on pay has come from the cash limits system. In 1975, Healey made it clear that the major reason for introducing cash limits was a wish to impose a ceiling on pay rises in the public services (where there had recently been large rises to make up for the discriminatory suppression of state employees' pay under the previous incomes policy). The Treasury official responsible for the cash limits system told a committee of MPs in 1976 that 'in the absence of any other incomes policy, cash limits could be the incomes policy' – a potential which the Thatcher government seized on, with grateful acknowledgements to their predecessors. From 1975 to 1979 cash limits held down public employees' pay in line with a formal incomes policy which was less strictly applied in the private sector. Since then cash limits have been deliberately used as an uncompromising form of pay curbs in the public sector alone.

Cash limits are perfectly suited to this role since they pre-set limits on the permissible rise in the price of labour, which can only be changed through elaborate formal procedures which would involve a public retreat by government. This has happened on only one occasion, in 1979; it was politically possible because there was an intervening general election which allowed the Tories to increase their predecessors' cash limit without loss of face. This 'unwinding' process also carried over into the setting of the cash limits for 1980, which made some allowance for the operation of the various special reviews following the disputes of 1979. Apart from that occasion, cash limits have always assumed pay rises below the expected rate of inflation.

Once cash limits have been set, the only way of allowing pay rises above the figure is by cutting the volume of spending, either on labour or other factors: in other words, paying for the rise by job loss and/or cuts in services. Thus settlements in 1980, 1981 and 1982 were often slightly above the cash limit, but, since this was not changed, the settlements could only be financed by cuts elsewhere. The working class as a whole was not allowed to gain extra resources.

Pay has been attacked in other ways as well. Existing systems of pay negotiation and arbitration have been scrapped or weakened. One example is the suspension by Labour and the abolition by the Tories of the comparability machinery in the civil service. Another is the scrapping by the Tories of the right of teaching unions to go to arbitration without their employers' agreement. Yet another has been the breaking of established pay links, like those of health service white-collar staff to civil servants.

Low pay is as great a problem as ever. The Tories have declared that in their view low pay is of no concern to the employer: 'In general terms pay is a matter for the market and social needs are the province of the social security system', as they told the Civil Service Arbitration Board. Previous practice has not been all that different. In the 1960s it was decided that low pay among council workers should be dealt with by subjecting them to work-studied bonus schemes, thus linking pay to productivity. When school meals workers were studied, the employers found that they were *already* working as efficiently as possible. They did not, however, immediately offer them a maximum bonus: they concluded that since a bonus scheme could not increase productivity, the workers should not get any bonus at all.

While this kind of capitalist virtue was going unrewarded, some state employees were singled out for special treatment. In the period 1977–79 the police, the armed forces, the top state officials such as judges and Whitehall mandarins, and the doctors and dentists, were all given dispensation from the pay policy and received special increases from their own review bodies.

The attacks have not been confined to pay. Pressure on other conditions of service have also been a feature of the period, most notably in the persistent attempts to worsen the pension benefits – or increase the pension contributions – of public employees. School meals workers were again singled out by the employers, who began attempting in 1981 and 1982 to stop their retainer pay during the school holidays and return them to the status of casual labour. There have been a number of attempts to replace permanent employees by casual workers or teenagers on the Youth Opportunities Programme, most notoriously through the Work Experience scheme: such trainees have no job security, a minimal allowance instead of a wage, and no formal job responsibilities. The most extreme example of this has been the moves to replace paid workers with unpaid volunteers: one council started building kitchens for operation by the Women's Royal Voluntary Service, to replace school meals staff.

The privatisation of work by putting it out to contract has also been a key method for eroding conditions and job security. One effect of such proposals has been to force workers to accept reductions in hard-won conditions, such as pension rights, in attempts to keep their jobs.

Cut jobs, forget services

Getting rid of jobs has been an explicit objective of the cuts programmes of both Labour and Conservative governments since 1976. Both committed themselves to targets for reducing the number of civil servants, and both sought to force local authorities to do the same. Discussion of this issue by the media has been characterised by a curious willingness to accept without question that public employees do nothing and therefore will not be missed when they are sacked.

In practice, most of the measures adopted to cut jobs have directly or indirectly worsened public services. A good example is the cuts in education introduced in 1976. These decreed that the number of teachers would not after all be maintained at planned levels, because the number of children was expected to fall. The pupil/teacher ratio has traditionally been used as a measure of the quality of education provision: the fewer pupils to every teacher, the better. But, as an employer, the government was now saying the opposite: the worse the ratio, the more productive the teacher. This was made explicit by city stockbrokers Phillips and Drew who, in 1977, told investors in local authority bonds that education and social services staffing were crucial areas in which to demand reductions, quoting the pupil/teacher ratios in Coventry as 25.2 pupils per teacher in primary schools and 16.3 in secondary schools, and concluding bluntly that 'these are figures that must be increased if rapid and large scale cuts in spending are demanded'.

The crudest and probably most significant way of getting rid of public service jobs has been simply to provide less staff to do the work. In 1979, for instance, the Tories fixed them so that the services planned would have to be carried out by 3 per cent less staff than was originally viewed as necessary. This followed the practice of the previous government, which had called such adjustments 'good housekeeping'. The pressures to keep within cash limits, discussed in Chapter 5, ensured a further shortfall. The effects of this can be seen in Table 7 (see p. 111), which compares the official figures for the money actually spent on staff with the staffing assumed by the original plans in the estimates. The comparison indicates that from 1976–77 to 1980–81 there has been a 'productivity' gain averaging about 5 per cent per year. These figures relate directly to civil service workers, but since similar squeezes have operated on the NHS and local government they probably reflect the overall experience.

The impact of this kind of squeeze is completely unseen by those imposing the financial constraints. Despite government rhetoric about 'general incentive to economy and efficiency', it is about as sophisticated as a football club saving wages by fielding only ten players in the team and talking about 'improved workrates'. The reality can only be seen by looking at the daily work of a group of staff, something that politicians and top management are loath to do. In Kennington social security office, for example, the 'productivity squeeze' operated against a background of inner city deprivation – low incomes, poor housing, and soaring unemployment. By 1981 there were 103 claimants to every worker, compared with 77 per worker in 1976. The attempts to cope with this had nothing to do with urbane Whitehall platitudes about 'efficiency': staff were organised and reorganised to try and concentrate on the most urgent backlog, thus creating further backlogs in other areas. The appointments system was periodically abandoned, at one stage the office was closed to callers for a few days to try and catch up, and precise assessment of benefits took second place to pushing some money out to claimants, even if it was the wrong amount.

This sort of thing happened in hundreds of workplaces throughout the public services. When the process of implementing the squeezes is considered, it is totally unsurprising. The most common approach is simply to leave vacancies unfilled, either permanently or for a few months: indeed, in 1979 the government ordered a recruitment freeze to ensure that posts were left vacant. As a result, the shortage of staff is concentrated in the grades to which recruitment takes place, which are predominantly in the lower grades, and thus the pressure of increased workloads falls most of all on those most subject to management pressure to do more work to cover the gaps left by the unfilled posts.

The squeeze has led to cynical revisions by management of officially agreed procedures for determining staffing needs. For example, a detailed job analysis and work study programme had formed the basis for a formula which related the staff needed in Job Centres to the number of unemployed. Since cash limits did not allow for the full numbers required, the government simply divided the annual figures of staff needed by an arbitrary amount to make them fit the cash limit. By 1980, the resulting shortage of staff below requirements was estimated at about 10 per cent. In other parts of national government services, the staff formulae were fiddled by deducting allowances for breaks (a technique which has also enjoyed recent popularity with manufacturing companies).

Statistics used by management to monitor workloads – which are proudly trotted out to impress MPs and others – are equally distorted by the realities of pressure. Social security offices have their share of staff allocated according to the figures they keep of the number of cases dealt with. Yet the pressure of work itself means that these figures are often not fully recorded, if dealing with claimants is given priority, and an office which takes more time and care to give a decent response is actually penalised because its turnover of cases is lower – 'efficiency' is again linked to poor services.

The classic double-edged system is in Inland Revenue tax collection offices, where the number of outstanding letters to be dealt with are counted every month: these returns are added together by region and nationally, to show whether extra staff are needed. Apart from the fact that counting letters is no measure of how much time they take to deal with, the whole system is also used as a personal performance check – those individual clerks, supervisors and managers with no letters outstanding are rewarded with better promotion prospects, and an office manager trying to impress his or her supervisors can give a real ear-bashing to any unfortunate member of staff who has spoiled the statistics for that month. As a result, there is a comprehensive effort to fiddle the figures downwards, thus underestimating even the irrelevant measure of workload chosen. It is no coincidence that the press occasionally report finds of bundles of letters to the Inland Revenue in hedges or ditches. They are glimpses of the true face of management 'efficiency'.

A final illustration of how official 'productivity' has little to do with services and everything to do with exploiting labour is the government's approach to using new technology. There are wide potential applications in the public services, yet the official approach to such projects is based on a simple reduction in labour costs rather than an improvement in services. The classic example of this was a computerised system of matching jobs to job seekers which could have been of real use to the unemployed in London, and which won an award for the computer project most likely to be of social benefit. The Labour government insisted that the project was implemented solely to cut staff costs – 'protecting the taxpayer's interest' was the phrase used by Employment Minister Albert Booth – and it was finally abandoned by the Tory government after an agreement reached to redeploy staff rather than sack them was rejected by the Treasury as not yielding a sufficient return on investment.

Privatisation

The ultimate logic of the pressures on public service workers finds its clearest expression in the drive for privatisation. This has taken various forms, including the sale of nationalised assets like Amersham International or British Aerospace, the financial and political encouragement of private education and private medicine, and above all the drive to contract out to the private sector work which has previously been done by directly employed labour. Local council building work has to be put out to tender, with the financial terms arranged so that the councils' own building organisations are at a disadvantage. Street cleaning and office cleaning are other areas where contractors are being introduced to replace direct labour.

There has been large-scale public promotion of the image that private contractors are more efficient and so cheaper and better value. Even in its own terms it is often untrue. Councils which have examined the relative costs of the use of contractors have frequently concluded that the kind of savings claimed, for example, for Southend Council's privatisation of refuse and cleansing are artificially exaggerated. And the experience of some councils such as Islington with building contractors has shown heavy costs from delays, bankruptcies and shoddy work.

There are, however, real economic and political gains for employers from the use of private contractors. They erode the conditions and job security of workers, and they allow the extraction of profits from an area previously under state control. The cost reductions can be real enough: the key issue is not whether they are 'really' cheaper for the council establishment, but how their cost-cutting is done: at the expense of the workers. The use of contractors also further removes work from political control and responsibility.

One of the clearest illustrations of this is office cleaning. The contract cleaning industry employs about 200,000 people – nearly 1 per cent of Britain's employees. The overwhelming majority of them are women, and about half are from ethnic minorities. There are a large number of small firms, easily started and ended because little capital is required. Government departments have found that they are invariably cheaper than employing direct cleaners. This is not because the contractors have space-age vacuum cleaners that the government can't handle, but because of the conditions of employment they provide.

One way in which contractors cut costs is by underpaying their workers. Despite an official agreement that cleaners must be paid the local authority rate, at least 9 per cent of cleaners on government contracts are paid less. One firm, when challenged by a department for not paying the agreed rate, replied with disarming honesty that it couldn't afford to do so. Moreover, private firms make a financial gain of 5½ per cent by not paying the normal civil service allowance for night-work, and whereas the civil service allows a half-hour break for every three-and-a-half hours worked, private firms are less generous. Every hour paid for is working time. And the very concept of hours is a flexible one for contract cleaners, due to the practice of 'job and finish'. This arrangement is frequently said to be in the interests of the workers, but firms aim to time jobs so tightly that the 'typical worker' will always need to work the full hours on which the contract is based – if not longer.

Private firms also gain a competitive edge by not providing any pension rights for their employees. This compares with the 14 per cent cost of superannuation for government cleaners – a right they won in 1971 after a successful fight to include part-time workers in the civil service pension scheme. Low pay and short hours also mean that there is no danger of firms having to pay into the state earnings-related pension scheme either.

Short hours have a further advantage. Nearly 90 per cent of cleaners work fewer than 16 hours a week, as a result of which they are not covered by many of the provisions of the Employment Protection (Consolidation) Act, 1978. So no claims for unfair dismissal can be made.

Wasteful practices such as paid holidays and sick leave are also curbed by the entrepreneurs. After one year's service, cleaners get less than one week's holiday from half the firms in the business; after two years' loyalty, a third of the firms still give one week or less, while a generous 54 per cent of firms give up to two weeks. As for sick leave, 89 per cent give no sick pay at all to part-time cleaners. Instead, holidays and sickness are often dealt with by a system known as 'covering'. This involves the absent worker finding a friend or relative to cover the job during the period of absence, and transferring all payment to the 'cover'.

The other major technique for reducing costs in the private sector is to make the workers do more for their money. One contractor bid for a government job on the basis that each cleaner would deal with 2,400 square feet per hour, compared with the civil service norm of 1,500 square feet. This figure (2,400 square feet) is about the floor area of an average semi-detached house, and the cleaner's job involves vacuuming, sweeping or mopping the entire floor area; dusting and dry-polishing all furniture; dusting all ledges, pipes and skirtings; dusting telephones and lampshades; emptying and cleaning ashtrays and glasses; cleaning lavatories, sinks and mirrors; and disposing of rubbish to collection points. This kind of work rate is sweated labour, and it is not surprising that contract cleaners are notorious for poor quality work.

The nearest contractors come to saving money by their own ingenuity is by employing their workers for fewer hours each week than does the civil service. They thus avoid having to pay National Insurance contributions, since their employees' weekly pay falls below the lower earnings limit. This saves the firm 13.7 per cent of the wages bill. The government obviously loses an equal amount of revenue, and yet the Treasury refuses to take this into account in valuing contractors' prices. They do so on the enlightened grounds that the loss of contributions is balanced by the fact that the workers concerned will no longer be entitled to any benefits. So it is again the workers who pay for this 'cost efficiency'.

There is, however, a slight difficulty with replacing direct labour by contractors; the government has to pay 15 per cent VAT on the contractor's price. But this is ignored in the costings – because, says the Treasury, the VAT simply returns to the state as revenue and so there is no net cost. The Treasury actually felt the need to issue a special circular on this subject, so that departments were not put off contractors by this cost. Yet there is every reason why they should be, since cash limits treat VAT payments on a par with all other spending. The VAT paid on new cleaning contracts therefore has to be found by making cuts in other department services.

Other work put out to contractors shows a similar pattern. Building workers or street cleaners get far worse conditions from the private firms, which, in turn, profit from the lower costs. Labour discipline is also far more primitive. Pritchards for instance, who took over the street cleansing in Wandsworth, have sacked workers instantly for spending 15 minutes too long on a tea-break. Unions are not encouraged.

Summary

The contrast between the establishment view of public employees and socialist concepts of the dignity of labour and the value of public services, could not be more marked. To the establishment such workers are costly, unproductive, and in need of the labour discipline of the private entrepreneur to be made profitable. Reduction in labour costs, under the guise of efficiency is given political priority over any political commitment either to workers or services.

The attack on state workers has brought a strong response from the workers themselves. They have not been, however, part of the mainstream of the established labour movement. The next chapter looks at the alternative strategies developed by that movement to see whether the interests of workers and services are reflected in them.

8.

Alternative Strategies

The cuts have met with resistance. The fightback has been spearheaded by campaigns and direct action. These important developments are examined in the next chapter. This one looks at influential arguments put forward on the left and at alternative economic strategies proposed. It evaluates them in the light of the cuts machine described in previous chapters.

Some arguments

One form of opposition to the cuts has been counter-propaganda, in the shape of arguments against the publicly advanced justification for cuts. The general arguments are reviewed and summarised here, although other arguments have also been advanced in relation to specific services. These general positions fall into a handful of broad categories.

International comparisons. One approach has been to set out comparisons of the level of public spending, public borrowing, and taxation in Britain and other western countries. These comparisons have consistently shown that the percentage of Gross National Product taken in tax in Britain is about average, and that the level of public sector borrowing in relation to Gross National Product has been fairly typical.

These facts have been used against the crudest form of propaganda for cuts, which has stated that Britain is spending beyond its means, is taxed too heavily, and is borrowing profligately. The weakness of these crude images has been the absence of any clear standards by which the level of spending and so on are to be judged. It was apparently received wisdom in the Treasury in the mid-1970s that if public spending rose to 60 per cent of GNP or more, then democracy was threatened. This ludicrous product of establishment paranoia was treated with equally ludicrous respect by the media, until international comparisons helped force it out of respectable political discussion.

The borrowing argument was similarly put in perspective – how much borrowing was acceptable, and why? If such countries as Japan could borrow more than Britain without disaster ensuing, what standard was being used when first Labour Chancellor Healey and then Tory Chancellor Howe fixed on £11 billion per year as some magic ceiling? No rational answer was forthcoming – the standard being used was the 'confidence' of the financial markets, which had little to do with any reasoned judgement about the economic interests of the British people.

So too with taxation. Although the burden of taxation has been redistributed between various groups, the overall level in Britain is low for European countries – so why should taxes be so damaging to the 'incentives' that British executives apparently needed? The facts did not hinder the Healey propaganda of 1976, nor the Tory election campaign of 1979. But they again raised effective questions about the rationality of such arguments.

Financial management. Another set of arguments for the cuts focused on finance. Public borrowing was taking funds away from industry and the cost of debt interest was growing too high. So cuts were necessary both to allow businesses more scope for raising money, and to reduce costs.

The first of these arguments has been simply refuted by opponents of the cuts. Industry was not desperate for finance at any time during this period, as was indeed admitted by both the Treasury and the CBI in 1977, in evidence to the Wilson Committee. Moreover, there was no reason to assume that there was a limited pool of finance which the government and industry were competing for, unless the government itself placed an artificial limit on domestic credit as part of its monetarist policy. This point too was admitted by a Tory minister in evidence to a Commons Select Committee in 1981.

The second argument about the cost of debt interest has also been refuted on a number of grounds. The forecasts of this interest, which was an important part of the case for the 1976 cuts, was shown to be heavily exaggerated – and the unjustified weight given to it was subsequently partly recognised by a revision of the definition of debt interest, producing a much smaller figure. In any case, the *real* cost of government debt was zero or less, because inflation was eroding the cost of capital repayments. Moreover, the cuts themselves created unemployment, and so actually added to the level of public expenditure and borrowing (because of higher benefit payments and lower tax receipts). The use of this last argument, it should be noted, has sometimes caused new problems, leading in turn to the Tory response that benefits should be reduced – and taxed – as a way of increasing the 'incentive' to work, and to the further demand for cutting wages so that the 'cost' of public sector employment becomes more acceptable – i.e. closer to the cost of keeping someone unemployed.

Resources. Another variant of the official case that the swollen public sector was 'crowding out' industry was that it was preempting resources that industry needed. The response to this has been to point out vigorously that industry has not been seeking to employ more labour, that any labour shortages that existed were for very specific skills in very specific areas which did not correspond in any way with the kind of labour being shed by the public services as a result of the cuts. In fact, the expansion of public service employment (until the late 1970s) in all western countries, has been vital in making up for the fact that the steady rise in productivity has reduced industry's need for labour, even during times of growth.

Reduced demand. Another key argument presented as a public justification for the cuts is that 'the country' can't afford to 'live beyond its means'. To spend more on public services it must produce more, and not borrow irresponsibly to make up the deficit. The response to this has been to emphasise that it is both natural and necessary for government borrowing to be at a high level during recession in order to maintain demand and employment throughout the economy – one of the classic tenets of Keynesian economics. To cut public spending simply increases and intensifies the recession and thus worsens unemployment. Recent arguments from the TUC have placed special emphasis on the economic interrelation of the public and private sectors, and the nonsense of treating them as separate.

Inflation. To the monetarists the major reason for cutting public spending is that government borrowing is inflationary – it amounts to printing money. Two main arguments have been made in response. First, that the cuts themselves have been major inflationary factors, by the prevalent use of increasing nationalised industry prices, charges for school meals, etc., as well as reducing subsidies: and the Tory tax cut strategy in 1979 put up VAT which increased the retail price index by nearly 4 per cent. The disarming John Biffen blithely told a Commons Committee that this was not, in his view, inflationary just because it put up prices: 'real' inflation was only what increased the money supply. This defence demolishes monetarism by the age-old technique of *reductio ad absurdum*. More technically, and on the monetarists' own territory, it has been demonstrated that the PSBR has in fact contributed very little to the growth of the money supply in recent years: its financing has been largely and increasingly 'non-inflationary', whilst the major source of monetary growth has been bank borrowing by the private sector.

Burden of cuts. The core of most opposition to the cuts has centred around a critique of their effects. By increasing unemployment, increasing the prices of essentials, and cutting the collective provision of services, workers and families were being made to pay for the economic crisis. It has also often been pointed out that these cuts were being made in order to restore the profitability of businesses, and hence were a clear class issue.

Which alternative? The relative emphasis placed on these arguments has indicated the kind of political response supported. To simplify, the strongest advocates of the 'demand' arguments, have tended to advocate an alternative governmental policy based on reflation of the economy. Concern with the arguments about the burden of cuts has tended to be most associated with supporters of active political campaigning. The rest of this chapter examines the 'official' labour movement position, presented in the 'alternative economic strategy' (AES).

Keeping cash limits

The AES has been developed since the mid-1970s, as a result of disillusionment with the policies of the post-1974 Labour government. It stems from various sources, including proposals from some public service unions at that time for an alternative to cuts. But its central concern has always been the 'regeneration of British industry', and this is reflected in how little most versions of the AES have to say about public services. Rather than spell out yet another general critique of the AES, it is considered here in the light of what is said about three key political aspects of the cuts machine: cash limits, the value of services and the absence of democratic controls.

One good test of people's attitude to public services is what they say about cash limits. These, as previously argued, subordinate services to finance and automatically incorporate pay restraint as a prime policy goal.

The first TUC *Economic Review* published after the introduction of cash limits (1976) had nothing to say about them. In 1977, the annual Congress carried overwhelmingly a motion which called for the ending of cash limits as an unacceptable form of pay policy – but only after the General Council had been divided on the issue, and taken the unusual step of making no recommendation. Len Murray did, however, warn that 'the public purse is not bottomless', which presumably indicated more than a passing sympathy with the cash limits principle.

The 1978 *Economic Review* seemed to be fairly bold in its opposition. Expressing concern about the underspending caused by cash limits, it asserted that 'it is imperative that an alternative to the cash limit system of public expenditure control is begun to be devised', and complained of 'the over-rigid implementation of cash limits'. But by 1979, just before the election, cash limits warranted only a passing mention (as a problem for pay negotiations). Judging by the 1980 and 1981 *Reviews* the main problem with cash limits was their effect on nationalised industries. There was no call for their abolition, merely one for 'a new financial framework' for these industries.

Congress in 1980 and 1981 again passed motions calling for an end to 'the system of cash limits', but some leading General Council members made clear that they interpreted this as calling for 'a different system of cash limits'. The 1982 *Review*, in criticising the new system of cash planning, referred to the established problem of underspending resulting from cash limits, but commented that 'a government which was serious about meeting these [volume] targets could have made good any gap between the cash limit based on a forecast of prices for the year ahead and the actual level of prices in that year', implying that there is nothing inherently wrong with a cash limit system.

In February 1982 TUC evidence to the Treasury and Civil Service Select Committee finally spelt out the official view. On the basis of a highly dubious historical account (of which more below) it said:

> Essentially, therefore, the TUC wishes cash limits to be set to allow for forecast inflation . . . and for any shortfall to be made good through supplementary estimates and roll-over provisions. Cash limits should not be used as a means for cutting public expenditure, or attempting to contain inflationary pressures, but as an instrument to help fulfil expenditure programmes [sic]. Measures to contain inflation and to ensure that costs in the public sector do not rise inordinately would need to be agreed following the National Economic Assessment and should be quite distinct from the operation of cash limits.

This position is politically objectionable. In the first place, it is quite different from the policies decided by Congress, which has called for the abolition of cash limits. An undemocratic policy is invariably a serious weakness in the trade union movement, and it suggests that the TUC bureaucracy has positive reasons for *not* wanting the abolition of cash limits.

In the second place, it is based on gross factual and historical misconceptions. The evidence to the Select Committee claims:

> cash limits were introduced originally as a means of providing standard guidance about the kind of levels of inflation that could be expected over a given year – cash limits did not rule out any supplementary increases to accommodate unforeseen changes in the costs of programmes. It was also envisaged that any shortfall in terms of estimates of inflation below actual outturn could be made good in the subsequent annual estimates.

This is complete nonsense. As pointed out in Chapter 5, cash limits were originally introduced by a Labour government, just as they were putting together an incomes policy with the TUC in 1975, explicitly to fix cash limits on public sector wage bills and as a means of controlling public expenditure in the short term (Denis Healey, July 1975). Guidance had nothing to do with it. And the new system was distinguished from what had happened previously precisely because it did *not* envisage that under-estimates of inflation would be 'made good in subsequent estimates'. As practical experience has confirmed, the whole point of the system was to avoid this.

The third major problem with the TUC's position is the presumption that it is necessary to have measures 'to ensure that costs in the public sector do not rise inordinately'. Since the biggest category of public sector costs is pay, these measures are likely to imply pay curbs, and presumably other 'guidance' to public administrators on acceptable price levels, and if such measures are enforced administratively it is difficult to see how they would differ from cash limits, which were designed precisely to curb 'inordinate' rises in public sector costs.

The objective is, in practice, indistinguishable from cuts in services and workers' pay and conditions. As the TUC themselves point out the public services are only valued in terms of their own costs, and so it is not practical under current systems to distinguish curbs on costs from cuts.

The 1982 joint Labour Party/TUC document, *Economic Planning and Industrial Democracy*, gives the cash limits system the same status as incomes policy, by supporting it under a euphemistic disguise. Thus paragraph 73 slips in 'Clearly, within the five-year rolling period covered by PESC it will be necessary for the Treasury to carry out annual monitoring of Departmental spending and exercise short-term financial control.' Put more simply: 'Cash limit controls will continue.'

In contrast to the TUC the public service unions have been fairly consistent. In 1977, the National Steering Committee of public service unions called for immediate action to reverse most cuts, and argued that immediate action was possible to restore major cuts, and insisted on the need 'above all, to replace the system of cash limits, which had had such a damaging effect on the public services'. The same unions reiterated this view in January 1979: 'Cash limits must be ended. They have no defensible role in a balanced democratic system of planning.' But there was still some equivocation: NALGO state on the same page of a 1979 policy document that their policy was 'that the cash limit system should be abolished', and continue that 'there is a strong case for the extension of collective bargaining to include the settling of those cash limits, and the assumptions and premises on which they are drawn up.' This latter, more limited objective has also been pursued by the civil service unions, and was indeed won as a guarantee following the 1981 strike. But in practice the assumption of a 4 per cent pay rise was set by the government before the 1982 negotiations ever started, and there was no negotiable reason for them to change them.

The academic advocates of the AES have little to say about cash limits, although one (D. Cobham) has stated baldly:

cash limits . . . cannot usefully be regarded merely as an underhand way of implementing further expenditure cuts, for the problem they were designed to face was and is a serious one, and would be faced by any left government trying to operate the AES since aggregates such as the budget deficit, the PSBR and the 'real' level of public expenditure itself are central to any macro-economic

policy. These problems of control must therefore be taken
seriously if the AES is to have any credibility.

It appears to be assumed by advocates of the AES that public
services are, unless watched very carefully, inflationary was-
trels. The Treasury convention that public employees cannot
improve their productivity is formally rejected (e.g. by the
TUC), but is indirectly assumed in discussions of the relative
merits of public services and industry. The assumption that
public service output is not 'wealth' is rejected but re-emerges
as the observation that it is not 'tradeable', and so remains of
lesser value.

Valuing services

So what value do proponents of the AES put on the public
services? As they point out, the AES is not about attaining
socialism, but primarily about regenerating British industry and
restoring growth to the British economy. It thus shares the
stated objectives of the Labour government of the late 1970s,
which placed a similar priority on industrial revival.

In this scheme of things, the crucial role of public spending is
as an instrument for injecting more demand into the economy.
Thus the 1981 *Economic Review* argued: 'Public spending
must be used to boost output and employment in all sectors of
the economy. It could also be used to improve the quality of
life.'

Similarly, the London CSE group, arguing that campaigns
against cuts are negative and divisive, has urged a *positive* case
for public spending. It sees it as vital for four quite different
reasons. First, it 'serves to raise the level of demand in the
economy'; second, it creates jobs; third, it contributes to living
standards; and finally, it challenges the market. But the thrust
of the book reinforces the view that the demand-creating role is
by far the most important. Thus the 'basic elements' of the
AES are said to include 'a policy for expansion aimed at
restoring full employment and raising living standards, based
on a planned reflation of the economy, primarily through increases in public spending.'

This demand-creating role implies an emphasis on capital spending. The TUC programmes outlined in both 1981 and 1982 *Economic Review* give most weight to capital projects. In *The Road from Thatcherism* Sam Aaronovitch agrees that 'capital spending should be increased at a much faster rate than current spending, given that the former is, of course, much smaller than the latter.' There are many good reasons of social need for spending money on building houses, and schools, but these reasons are secondary in the AES. The main point is to boost demand for the construction industry.

This secondary role given to public services is characteristic of the AES. Although its supporters explicitly reject the view that services are less productive than industry, they argue that industry is economically more important because its products are traded and, according to some, because it has more potential for increasing productivity and hence growth. Hence the priority of the AES is managing resources to get industrial growth, and the expansion of public services is largely dependent on this growth. In all versions, it is emphasised that the AES must take seriously the problem of how to *finance* increased public spending, and the key long-term answer is from growth and North Sea oil, defence cuts and higher borrowing.

There is an awful familiarity about arguments like this:

> More resources will be needed for exports and investment . . . further improvements in our public services depend on our industries generating the output and overseas sales to make these improvements possible. North Sea oil will make an important difference to our affairs, but it will not be big enough by itself . . . we must improve the quality of other industries.

The quotes could be from an AES pamphlet but are, in fact, from the White Paper of February 1976 with which the last Labour government launched its massive series of cuts. AES supporters are very different politically from Denis Healey, but the problem for the public services is that their strategy points to the same priorities in practice. What if a government committed to the AES finds that the projected rise in public spending has 'not been matched by the growth in output', which the

AES aims to be 4 per cent a year. If the economic value of public services depends on their contribution to industrial regeneration, then the prospects are bleak.

Non-industrial democracy

What proposals does the AES have for democratising control of the public services? *Industrial* democracy is central to most versions of the AES, including workers' representation on company boards and the requirement for companies to reach planning agreements with their workers within the framework of a national planning assessment. But no versions have similar demands for the public services.

The CSE version, for instance, does not even mention the question of control of the public services, and so presumably regards it as irrelevant to the AES. Sam Aaronovitch, on the other hand, devotes much space to calling for services to be made accountable to the communities they serve, and for giving workers a say in how those services function. He envisages building from cuts campaigns to demands for such democratisation, and criticises bureaucratic concentration on planning resources rather than services.

But even these objectives would leave the public services subordinate to a national Department of Planning, which would be concerned with the 'shares' of national income which should go to investment, personal consumption, or collective consumption – but which would not have actual control over 'national income'.

The TUC has more detailed proposals. These originated with ideas advanced by public sector unions in 1979, which criticised the system of planning public spending as closed, secretive, and undemocratic. They called for involvement of relevant unions at all stages in the process, publication of information, and positive valuation given to employment as part of public service planning.

The TUC's position focuses on the involvement of unions and in particular the TUC. There is to be an overall National Economic Assessment, involving government, the TUC and the CBI. The PESC system would then be opened up by relevant unions being involved 'in working out detailed needs and plans'. This is expanded to indicate that the National Economic Assessment would produce the guidelines for the PESC planning process: that departmental reports would be drawn up with unions, and published, and that cabinet decisions would then involve discussions with the TUC, and the earlier union involvement 'would allow for a balanced view both on levels of expenditure and priorities for programmes within it'. The process would, at all stages, 'spell out implications for the quality of services provided and the implications for employment'. The TUC is quite clear about what this means:

> The TUC accepts that, for it to play a useful role in the PESC process, it will need itself to take vigorous views on the expenditure priorities and medium term social and economic strategies . . . the TUC as a whole, might have different priorities for public expenditure as compared to the health service unions who would, inevitably, always be pressing for some expansion of the NHS . . . NHS unions would need to feed in their bids through some form of TUC machinery.

Finally, the TUC emphasises that it does not wish to see 'over centralised and bureaucratic forms of planning'. It envisages trade unions feeding in ideas and plans from their members. The role of the National Economic Assessment would then be to 'provide a framework' for decision-making.

These kinds of proposals could add significantly to the opportunities for political pressures on the system, through the release of information and through the formal chance for unions to submit views and proposals. These would be a definite gain.

But they would leave the basic problems untouched. The National Assessment would do exactly what the Treasury Assessment now does; that is, decide on the 'shares' of spending required by private industry, consumers and public services, despite having no control over the private sector, with the key priorities being the regeneration of industry and economic performance. It is difficult to see how the TUC involvement would alter the 'residual' role of public services.

Indeed, the TUC would wholeheartedly embrace this role in deciding priorities both for the economy as a whole and within 'public expenditure'. It is hard to see, especially with a continued system of cash limits, how the envisaged involvement of unions can succeed in injecting the 'needs of services' into this framework, except perhaps by volunteering more 'efficient' methods of operation. The system would still treat services as 'public spending'. It is even harder to see how the proposals could be anything other than centralised and bureaucratic, since it would all stem from the 'framework' of the tripartite National Economic Assessment.

The proposals in the TUC/Labour Party document *Economic Planning and Industrial Democracy* have the same defects. The system outlined there would appear to be somewhat more public, but poor old public services are still left fighting for the leftovers. The new-style National Planning Council will prepare the 'basic medium-term economic projection and proposals about expenditure priorities.' Then the old-style PESC exercise commences, under these guidelines, with the Treasury responsible (para 77) and involvement of workers limited to helping draw up the guidelines for inter-departmental bargaining. Then the cabinet would make the allocation decision between departments and the Treasury exercises the cash limit controls (para 77). The Treasury loses its economic forecasting role but retains, virtually unchanged, its control over public spending.

Summary

The way the AES treats public services is heartbreaking. They remain a problem of financing, a residual in the arithmetic of capitalism. Worse, there is a political defeatism about the AES's acceptance of the cuts machine as an appropriate tool of economic management. If the AES is ever disseminated widely enough to be discussed in detail by the people it is to effect, they will search in vain for some indication that the strategy rates social need above private profit.

9.

Conclusion

Issues and action

The issues raised by the cuts machine could not be more central to socialism. They concern the control of resources for need rather than for profit, the planning of services for the benefit of workers and communities rather than for business, and an open political democracy. Cuts are not made as a regrettable temporary measure in the interests of all, but because the problems of capitalism demand them.

Demands that society should be organised for need and not for profit have always been central to socialist politics. But the adoption of Keynesian economic strategies and the persistence of the male industrial worker as the embodiment of labour movement concerns have temporarily pushed them to one side. Public services have become engines of reflation, rather than the foundations of a fair society. Private capital has been rehabilitated by the AES as British industry, and political struggles to reduce its power over people's lives have been subordinated to strategies which seek to restore its vigour and profitability, and which appeal to the protection of traditional male job structures. A Labour government and the TUC nearly killed off child benefits for the crime of snatching money from men's wallets.

A socialist approach to public services should begin by asserting that the needs of people are paramount, and that the value of services is to be measured by the extent to which they meet those needs, and not by the financial burden imposed on business. It has to assert that the jobs, pay and working conditions of those working in the services are of central importance, not a cost to be reduced by getting as much out of them for as little as possible. It must demand that services are geared to ensuring that society does not lean on female domestic servitude. It has to affirm that workers and communities can and must have control of these services.

None of this makes any sense under the present control system. Valuing services by people's needs, and not by the 'unprofitable' cost of financing them, runs directly contrary to the official accounting and planning systems. Making the interests of the workers a primary objective is the reverse of present 'commercially sound' practices which treat jobs and pay as unproductive costs to British industry – and a reversal of the presumption that public servants are second-class workers. Insisting on democratic controls challenges the system of secret, central bureaucratic power exercising a restraining influence on dangerously unbusinesslike activities.

Many workers and communities have opposed the values of the present system. Public services should, in their view, serve economic and social needs. There is no problem about identifying or measuring or evaluating these *needs*: people know when they are in lousy housing, or with inadequate money or in need of treatment. The problem is that these needs are often not met, and that the authorities often work harder at cutting costs than accepting political responsibility for meeting needs. Workers' experience is even sharper. Low pay, limited resources and official indifference to services produce a constantly demoralising squeeze on workers and work alike.

Demands for public services based on socialist principles are not abstract. They are implicitly raised in dozens of fights against the cuts. Every time a hospital closure is fought, health workers and local people are demanding that the NHS should not simply enshrine the great principle of health care for all, according to need, but that it should be controlled by the people it serves and the workers it employs. When social security workers and claimants oppose the use of harassment, or of racist or sexist categories to deny people benefits, they are demanding that a social benefit system should be run by workers and the community to provide for local needs. When public service workers strike for pay, or take action against cuts in jobs, they are affirming the principle that a decent income and working conditions are fundamental rights – not an irritating cost to the lords of the economy.

Such fights are often dismissed as of limited value, concerned 'only' with local issues or with the 'narrow' self-interest of workers. One correct reply is that socialism is about serving the interests of communities and workers. Another is that the accusation that public employees only act on 'narrow' self-interest is untrue. Hospital ancillary workers took direct action in the mid-1970s against private practice in hospitals: the self-interest of those involved would certainly have been better served by shutting up and keeping their noses clean. In other cases, the 'limited' interests of the workers concerned may have sparked off the action, but the demands broadened as the dispute continued. One such case was in Islington in 1982, where all-out strike action by NALGO council workers began over the dismissal of one temporary worker, and continued for a further two weeks over the closure of a children's home.

Nor are such struggles conducted in isolation. Links between the users of services and workers are growing. For example, in Oxford in 1982, social security workers went on strike demanding more staff to handle claimants' problems. This strike received the full backing of the claimants' union, which was already campaigning against harassment.

Similar links are being forged in campaigns against privatisation. Because the quality of contract work is usually far worse than that done by direct labour, tenants' groups have begun insisting that direct labour should be used to build and maintain housing. There is equally a recognition by public service workers that political support depends on a commitment on their part to running public services with the minimum of hassle for the public.

Such organised action not only poses a potential challenge to the system. It has already resulted in a number of victories. Cuts under the last Labour government were less than those sought by the cabinet, and employment in public services was at least maintained until 1980. Active opposition was crucial.

It was the ancillaries' action at Charing Cross hospital which forced a response from the Labour Secretary of State, Barbara Castle: her subsequent memoirs make clear that she saw it as an inconvenient interference with her cosy negotiations with the medical profession, by forcing private practice to be taken seriously as a political issue. The NALGO action in Islington was a fight against the first SDP council in Britain, which was later completely rejected at the elections.

Such battles are the spearhead of socialist opposition to the cuts machine. They raise the key issues of the valuation and democratisation of services and they create organised political pressures on the system. By contrast, TUC proposals (or even action) to reflate the economy through greater public spending, however desirable, do not confront these issues directly. The argument remains confined within the straitjacket of a loaded system – what level of public borrowing can 'the country' afford? The supporters of such proposals risk finding themselves stranded if international financiers remain unconvinced by their policy papers. The experience of 1976 does not suggest that rational argument persuades the money markets. Finally, the AES demand for a higher PSBR to reflate the economy is unlikely to grip the hearts and minds of the masses.

Strengthening the position of organised communities and workers is vital to changing the present system. Getting more enlightened helmspeople to steer the ship of state is no more (and no less) of an advance than getting enlightened personnel management in private companies. Neither alters the system fundamentally. Neither is a substitute for rank-and-file trade union and political organisation. The need for strong unionism is as great in the public services as in industry.

Some possibilities

These kinds of struggles are the seeds of a socialist programme for the public services. The values of collective caring are alive and kicking in the best of today's campaigns. And the lessons are not being lost. Union education programmes in the public services now include sessions on planning and controlling services. Some Labour councils are encouraging the development of 'bottom-up' planning. The recognition of the possible role of workers has even extended to managements wanting to make cuts, who frequently find that they depend on workers to explain to them how the services they want to cut operate.

Democratic alternatives could harness the potential shown in these examples. Instead of secret central financial planning, there should be a system which *starts* from what workers and communities want in their localities. The first input to the planning of housing services should be the damp patch on the wall of No. 24, the homelessness of Judy Brown, and the jobs and conditions of local building workers. Through tenants' organisations and union branches, people would work out what they saw as the problems and what kind of services they would value. Health plans could be started through community health councils *organising* people to express their demands for health services, and health workers doing the same through their unions (which would only be a belated extension of the incorporation of doctors' organisations into key positions in the health services). Local women's groups should put forward demands on jobs, child care, social services, etc. Claimants' groups and social security staff should work out what benefits are needed. And so on.

This need not wait on a dramatic restructuring of health authorities, government departments or the like. It could start with legislation which restated what most people erroneously believe to be the case: that their function is to provide services and their responsibility is to the people they are providing it to. This would clarify the new political priorities. Their planning role would be an exercise in listening to local demands and translating them into local plans for services, and subsequently into national ones. Their role would also be partly technical, in working out ways of delivering what is required. Officials who have become over-accustomed to working out reasons for not delivering what people want might need some retraining. One role would remain for proposals from national level, and that is laying down minimum standards for housing, education, income levels, child care and so on, to protect the working class of East Sussex and Buckinghamshire from extended deprivation by the locally dominant ruling class.

The end result would be a series of local and national plans which spelt out the services and employment that are demanded. The financing requirements should then be calculated on the basis of these plans, and the distribution of the burden should be worked out publicly, specifying the contribution to be made by business, by tenants, by landowners, and so on. The resulting 'budget' document would be presented not as a list of technical instruments but as an analysis of the class and group distributions resulting from original economic power and subsequent adjustments through taxation, rent and benefit plans. Raising the finance would then take the form of issuing tax demands and raising loans for specific services, thus emphasising the political nature of resistance to proposing such finance. Taxes for weapons would be separated from taxes for the NHS. The present system, described by the Treasury as traditional British practice, has the basic political disadvantage of isolating taxation from the services it supports.

The operation of services should then be monitored publicly, to ensure that what was planned was being done. The key things monitored would be services and jobs. The exercise would be carried out by workers and communities, to whom authorities and officials would be answerable. The existing financial information system would be retained for monitoring the money spent. Overspend and underspend would equally warrant investigation and political discussion of the appropriate response – which could be supplementary tax or rate demands. Workers in the services would play a key role because of their experience and obvious concern for the future of their services.

Most of the present system could be scrapped. Cash limits, cash planning and the Public Expenditure Survey cycle would have no role. They are purely administrative creations designed to curb public services. Even the PESC system, which is viewed with nostalgia by many in the Labour movement, was a way of politically subordinating services to business interests.

The structure and effects of the taxation system would also be more clearly exposed to public pressure, which is more important than any specific tax changes. The system of local rating should be changed to tax on a property ownership, rather than occupation. This could be supplemented by a Rate Support Grant which simply matched local rates in a 2 for 1 ratio, together with a stronger redistributive element. The key point is not which authority has the kudos of being able to raise taxes, but to ensure that tax raising is a response to the need for services. It should have no control function. That task would be performed by public and political monitoring of services, jobs and spending.

One result of such a system would be the wasting away of the Treasury. Central allocation of a restricted pool of spending would have no part in the planning process. If taxes were raised for specific services, instead of as an amorphous financial penalty, then the role of central budgetary control would also disappear. There is no magic skill needed to work out how much tax is needed to finance a given level of services, nor to issue bonds which are backed by government guarantee.

Problems and reforms

The response of capitalists is, of course, the problem with such a programme. If finance was subordinated to the services needed by people, and the planning and provision of services was no longer subject to central control within an acceptable financial total, then a 'loss of confidence' would inevitably occur. The money markets would make it crystal clear that they were not prepared to finance that new level of public services. Industry would also insist that it was unable to produce the resources required. And there would certainly be a campaign mounted by multinational companies explaining that the 'ordinary' rate and tax payer could not afford it either.

Socialists have always faced these kinds of problems. Capital does not want socialism, and uses many weapons – including the cuts machine – to oppose it. Programmes can only state socialist objectives; political struggle is needed to win them.

Recognising the inevitability of fierce opposition at least ensures that the problems are not ducked. Pretending that it will not happen can only lead to the abandonment of socialist aims.

Most immediately, what kind of limited reforms should be demanded of a future Labour government? The key criterion is that they must encourage political organisation to extend, improve and democratise public services. They must remove institutional obstacles for demands for services, and eliminate the presumption that the financial needs of the capitalist economy are paramount. Such reforms don't all add up to socialism. But they can create far more favourable terrain for class struggle than exists at present.

* The whole system of planning public services should be made public. Inputs from workers and communities should be systematically encouraged. Official secrecy should be ended, and institutions turned around so that they respond to needs. A PESC system, with TUC involvement, would be neither open nor democratic.

* Both the planning and the monitoring system should be based on explicit statements of levels of services and employment, and not just finance. Even reversion to volume prices would not be an adequate substitute for such statements.

* Political decisions about whether to raise finance to provide services and employment should not be pre-empted by any form of cash limits. The problems and the politics of these decisions must be made public, and not taken against services by an administrative fix.

* Public and political formulation of plans for services should not be constrained by any predetermined financial totals, as has been the case in one form or another since PESC was introduced. If a planning cycle remains, then there should be no Treasury guidelines at the start, no Treasury fixing of plans before they are subject to final decision, and plans based on the needs for services should be published before any final cabinet decision. The Treasury could then advance all its financial arguments on behalf of the City and businesses, and the political choice finally made would then have to be explained publicly.

* 'Alternative' national accounts, spending plans and budget should be presented on a regular basis showing the distribution of economic power and resources, between corporations and workers and families, as well as between individuals, both before and after tax and benefits. The plans should set out spending by corporations and individuals on a par with public services, and final incomes likewise. If there are economic reasons under capitalism why company chairs should be paid hundreds of thousands of pounds, while people are kept homeless, then they need to be given fair and full prominence.

* Legislation is needed to clarify for all sections of the public services that the overriding duty is to provide services and that they are accountable to the public for this. It would be a major advantage if legislation on local councils explicitly clarified that their overriding responsibility was to the whole electorate for the provision of services, and not to 'ratepayers' for minimising the rates. It could also be helpful to amend the rules of parliamentary procedure so that MPs were enabled, if they chose, to press the case for public services, rather than being constitutionally bound to protect the wealthy from taxation.

* Pay and conditions of public service workers should be a matter for public collective bargaining.

* The role of the audit throughout the public services – central government, the NHS, and local councils – should clearly be restricted by law to certifying that there had been no corrupt misappropriation of money raised for services. It should not in any way be concerned with 'efficiency' or 'value for money'. By contrast, the role of central government in enforcing minimum standards of service should be extended and strengthened. Bodies similar to the schools inspectorate, with precise legislative remit to maintain standards, should be set up or strengthened in other areas.

* The Rate Support Grant should be restored to its earlier role of supporting the rates, and the paraphernalia of sanctions developed in recent years should be scrapped. If the City wants cuts it can support Tory candidates. Charges such as rents and fares should be explicitly aligned with taxation and rates as a source of finance, rather than continuing to be treated as a

reduction in spending. Similar practices should be adopted for other services, such as the NHS.

* Reform of local government finance should concentrate on changing the application of rates away from occupiers and onto owners of property, rather than on changing the bureaucratic location of authority to raise particular forms of tax. A similar approach should be taken with national taxes, with tax reliefs being treated on the same basis as grants.

Last words

All this needs to be kept in perspective. Exposing the workings of the capitalist method of controlling public spending, and even mobilising against it, has to be part of a wider struggle. As a 1929 Labour Research Department pamphlet put it: 'Permanent victory for direct labour can only be won in a struggle extending along the whole front and ending with the establishment of the working class in power locally and nationally.'

In this light, perhaps the most encouraging political development of recent years is the growth of political awareness and militancy in trade unionists in the public services. Union fights over public services, and the links built with communities in these fights, are a significant extension of traditional British trade unionism, in the direction recommended by Marx:

> If the trade unions are required for the guerilla fights between capital and labour, they are still more important as *organised agencies for superseding the very system of wage labour and capital rule*. Too exclusively bent upon the local and immediate struggles with capital, the trade unions have not yet fully understood their power of acting against the system of wage slavery itself. They have therefore kept too much aloof from general social and political movements . . . Apart from their original purposes, they must now learn to act deliberately as organising centres of the working class in the broad interest of its *complete emancipation*. They must aid every social and political movement tending in that direction.

Tables

Table 1 **Changes in spending on public services, 1975–76 to 1983–84** (1975–76 = 100)

	Defence	Social security	All other
1975–76	100	100	100
1976–77	98·4	103·2	96·0
1977–78	96·2	108·6	89·6
1978–79	95·7	118·5	91·4
1979–80	98·5	121·4	91·2
1980–81	103·3	125·7	90·2
1981–82	103·3*	134·5*	87·2*
1982–83	106·5*	137·2*	83·9*
1983–84	109·7*	136·0*	81·4*

*Indicates *planned* expenditure.
Note These figures are based on constant price (volume) figures, and thus exclude the effects of changes in pay and price levels. They exclude the contingency reserve, allowance for shortfall, sale of assets, debt interest and nationalised industry borrowing from market and from government.
Source Calculated from Cmnd. 8175 (HMSO, 1981) Tables 1.7 and 1.9.

Table 2 **Hidden cuts resulting from cash limits, 1976–77 to 1980–81** (figures given as a percentage of annual budget)

	1976–77	1977–78	1978–79	1979–80	1980–81	1981–82
Defence						
underestimate of inflation*	−3	0	−3	−4	−2	−3
under/over spend**	−1·1	−1·5	+1·1	+2·4	+0·6	+2·7
Total squeeze	−4·1	−1·5	−1·9	−1·6	−1·4	−0·3
Other services						
underestimate of inflation	−3	0	−3	−4	−2	−3
underspend	−3·1	−3·0	−2·3	−1·9	−1·3	−3·3
Total squeeze	−6·1	−3·0	−5·3	−5·9	−3·3	−6·3

*Extent to which the assumptions built into the cash limits about the expected changes in pay and price levels underestimated the actual changes. These figures are given to the nearest whole number.

**The actual level of spending in relation to original cash limits (i.e. before any adjustments were made in anticipation of overspending). These figures are given to the nearest decimal place.

Sources Treasury and Civil Service Committee, HC 137 (Session 1981–82), Appendix 2; Cmnds. 7295, 7681, 7983, 8615 (HMSO; 1978–82).

Table 3 **Tax reliefs and grants, 1980–81** (figures given as £millions)

Group	Tax reliefs	Grants	Total
Private business	12,200	930	13,130
Pensioners	10	11,000	11,010
House owners	4,360	990	5,350
Children and women	180	4,500	4,680
Unemployed	490	3,300	3,790
Owners of capital	3,500	—	3,500
Sick and disabled	390	3,080	3,470
Nationalised industries	1,400	1,700	3,100
Married men	3,030	—	3,030
Council housing	—	2,250	2,250
Savers	1,740	—	1,740
Students	25	725	750

Note All figures relate to plans and projections for 1981 as set out in Cmnd. 8175. Grants have been revalued by about 10 per cent to convert them roughly to 1980–81 prices, for compatibility with tax reliefs.

The list of tax reliefs includes everything except the basic allowance for single persons, wives and the elderly. Value of relief to married men is the excess of the married man's allowance over the single allowance. Tax relief to private companies and nationalised industries includes relief on stock appreciation, investment, etc., and relief on petroleum revenue tax. Relief for capital gains on house sales is included under 'house owners'. Other reliefs are allocated to appropriate broad headings, e.g. relief on pensions and life insurances is allocated to 'savers'. The figures listed by the Treasury for tax relief on social security benefits have been followed, although short-term benefits are now taxable.

Redundancy and maternity fund payments are treated as grants to companies. Most of the MSC budget and special programmes are treated as grants to the unemployed. Grants to housing associations and the option mortgage scheme are allocated to 'house owners'. Transport grants are allocated to 'nationalised industries'. Agricultural support is not included in this table. Contributory benefits have been given as in Cmnd. 8175, without any adjustments for contributions paid.

Source Calculated from data in Cmnd. 8175 (HMSO, 1981) Tables 4.14, 2.12.1, 2.10, 2.7, 2.6, 2.4.

Table 4 **Class effects of budgets, 1979–82** (figures given as
　£millions)

	Effect on	
	all taxpayers	top incomes and business
1979	−1,025	+600
1980	+106	+386
1981	−2,463	+214
1982	+1,311	+2,177
Total	+2,071	+3,377

Note 'All taxpayers' are defined as the beneficiaries of changes in allowances, basic rates, and basic rate thresholds of income tax, and of all changes in indirect taxes.

'Top incomes and business' are defined as the beneficiaries of changes in higher rates or bands of income tax, in taxation of investment income, capital gains, capital transfer, corporation tax, etc. All figures relate to the effect in a full year.

The 1981 figures ignore £400millions windfall tax on banks, and treat failure to uprate personal allowances as worth zero, in line with budget presentation: in other years, increases in personal allowances are treated as gains to all taxpayers.

Source Calculated from *Financial Statement and Budget Reports* 'HMSO, 1979–82).

Table 5 **Real government borrowing, 1967–80** (figures given as
　£billions)

	Annual averages (calendar years)					
	1967–69	1970–72	1973–75	1976–78	1979	1980
Nominal PSBR	−0·9	−1·1	−7·0	−7·8	−12·6	−12·3
Real PSBR	+0·6	+1·9	+1·3	−0·1	+1·3	−0·2

Note 'Real PSBR' is after adjusting for the effect of inflation in reducing the value of debts.

Source: Bank of England Quarterly Bulletin, June 1981, pp. 232–34.

Table 6 **Functions and financing of government borrowing, 1976–77 to 1980–81** (figures given as £millions)

	1976–77	1977–78	1978–79	1979–80	1980–81
Total government borrowing	11,231	13,855	9,937	15,011	19,269
Functions					
repayment of debt	2,105	2,931	1,502	3,201	3,203
foreign currency deals	517	5,300	−622	1,142	815
financing companies	89	30	−101	765	2,059
PSBR	8,520	5,594	9,198	9,903	13,192
Financed by					
national savings	997	1,094	1,618	967	2,162
gilts	8,389	9,615	7,642	12,261	16,286
other	1,845	3,146	677	1,783	821

Sources Calculated from *Treasury Economic Progress Report* 136, August 1981, Table 2, and *Bank of England Quarterly Bulletin*, December 1981, Table 8.

Table 7 **Shortfall of staff in relation to workload in central government, 1976–77 to 1980–81** (figures given as a percentage of annual budget)

	1976–77	1977–78	1978–79	1979–80	1980–81
Staff cuts required by cash limit assumptions	−1·0	−1·3	−2·5	−5·0	−2·5
Underspend below cash limits*	−5·2	−5·4	3·7	−4·5	−1·3
Gross squeeze	−6·2	−6·7	−6·2	−9·5	−3·8
Offset by excess provision for staff in Estimates**	+2·1	+1·9	+1·3	+1·1	+1·0
Net squeeze	−4·1	−4·8	−4·9	−8·4	−2·8

*i.e. The actual level of spending in relation to original cash limits.
**i.e. Staff provided for in Estimates but not in post at the beginning of the financial year.
Sources: Cash Limit Outturns, Cmnd. 7295, 7681, 7983, 8437, 8615;
Memoranda on Supply Estimates, Cmnd. 6452, 6769, 7524, 7869, 8184.

A Guide to Reading

Chapter 1

A number of books have been written about economic problems and policies in the 1970s. One of the more readable ones is John Harrison and Andrew Glyn, *The British Economic Disaster*, Pluto Press 1980. Tougher going, but specifically focused on the cuts, is the CSE State Group's *Struggle over the State*, CSE Books 1979, which includes a detailed marxist discussion of the significance of the state. N. Bosanquet and P. Townsend (eds.), *Labour and Equality*, Heinemann 1980, is a collection of papers about the social policies of the Labour government from 1974 to 1979, which includes useful reviews of specific services as well as overview articles. Another collection which has some useful details of the impact of cuts on local government and health is D. Hood and M. Wright (eds.), *Big Government, Hard Times*, Martin Robertson 1981: the overview chapters, however, tend to look at the issue from the point of view of a dynamic executive making a career in public administration. The first year of Tory government is reviewed in a collection published by the Royal Institute for Public Administration, which is usefully comprehensive but of patchy quality – P. Jackson (ed.), *Government Policy Initiatives 1979–80*, RIPA, 1981.

On the more general question of the role of public services for a capitalist economy, which is not covered in this book, the outstanding account is Ian Gough, *The Political Economy of the Welfare State*, Macmillan 1979.

Accounts by active participants in the Labour government are available. They include L. Pliatsky, *Getting and Spending*, Basil Blackwell 1982, by a former civil servant centrally involved in the cuts of 1976, which is useful background to the official perception of the problem of public spending but unreliable on the precise structure of the events in 1976. The seminal expression of the argument that public spending was crowding industry is R. Bacon and W. Eltis, *Britain's Economic Problem: Too Few Producers*, Macmillan 1976.

Critical pamphlets on the cuts are numerous. Among the best and most accessible are various reports from Counter Information Services, 9 Poland Street, London W1. Useful union surveys of the cuts include National Steering Committee, *Breakdown: The Crisis in Your Public Services*, n.d. (1977); and Society of Civil and Public Servants, *The Advance of Decline*, SCPS 1980.

Information on public spending is published by the government each year in White Papers. The most recent are *The Government's Expenditure Plans, 1982–83 to 1984–85*, HMSO 1982, Cmnd.8494; and *The Government's Expenditure Plans 1981–82 to 1983–84*, HMSO 1981, Cmnd.8175. The latter is still useful since it is the last one to contain spending plans set out in constant prices, which enable more meaningful analyses to be made. The Labour White Paper which launched the cuts was *Public Expenditure to 1979–80*, HMSO 1976, Cmnd.6393. Other official publications with useful information are the reports of the House of Commons Treasury and Civil Service Committee (formerly the Expenditure Committee).

Detailed reports on all major developments are usually given in *The Financial Times*, and critical reports can be found in *Labour Research* from time to time.

Chapter 2

A clear exposition of the national accounts conventions affecting the treatment of the output of public services is given in a restricted NEDC paper *The Role of the Services Sector in the U.K.*, NEDC (81) 24. Some of the same points are summarised in the TUC's *Economic Review 1981*. A wide-ranging attempt to grapple with the problem of efficiency in the public services, from the point of view of making cuts, is in the Treasury and Civil Service Committee, *Efficiency and Effectiveness in the Civil Service*, HMSO, HC 236 (1981–82).

Official explanations of the conventions and basis of the National Accounts are reliably set out in *The National Accounts – A Short Guide* (Studies in Official Statistics, No.36), HMSO 1981. They can also be gleaned from the notes to each year's edition of *National Income and Expenditure*, HMSO, which update the original version in *National Accounts Statistics: Sources and Methods* (Studies in Official Statistics, No. 13), HMSO 1968.

The conventions adopted in public spending plans are set out in the notes to the annual White Papers. These have changed since the move from constant prices to cash as the basis for planning, and so the versions in both the 1981 and 1982 White Papers are worth examining (see notes to Chapter 1 for references). These also cross-refer to other explanations.

For an example of a discussion of the costs of unemployment simply in terms of the relative burden on the government's finances of employment and unemployment, see the House of Commons Social Services Committee, *Public Expenditure on the Social Services*, HMSO, HC 324 (1980–81).

Chapter 3

The best, and most readable, description of the tax system is J. Kay and M. King, *The British Tax System* (second edition), Oxford University Press 1980. It contains the authors' estimates of the tax paid by British companies in recent years, and a repeated insistence on the importance of the *effective* burden of taxation. Useful data on the impact of national insurance, and a summary of the relationship between personal taxation and the distribution of income and wealth is in Frank Field, *Inequality in Britain*, Fontana 1981: there is, however, virtually no discussion of the distribution of taxes between people and companies. A survey of the technical issues related to company taxation is contained in the government's green paper *Corporation Tax*, HMSO 1982, Cmnd.8456.

There is a large volume of recent literature on the rates. Useful historical material is contained in R. Foster, S. Jackman, and M. Perlman, *Local Government Finance in a Unitary State*, Allen & Unwin 1980. A classic exposition of the view that local democracy requires local taxation can be found in T. Burgess and T. Travers, *Ten Billion Pounds*, Grant MacIntyre 1980. The Tory government published a consultative paper on the rates, *Alternative to Domestic Rates*, HMSO 1981, Cmnd.8449, which summarises some of the alternatives canvassed and sets out some of their implications.

D. Jackson, H. Turner and F. Wilkinson, *Do Trade Unions Cause Inflation?* (second edition), Cambridge University Press 1976, is an influential work which highlights the distributive effects of taxation policies, and their relationship with distributional struggles through pay bargaining.

Official figures on taxation changes in the annual budget are published in the annual *Financial Statement and Budget Report*, HMSO. The value of tax reliefs are published as the final annexe in the annual White Paper on Public Expenditure. Details of the receipts from all taxes are given in the monthly *Financial Statistics*, HMSO. Data on rates and rateable values is available, for England and Wales, in the annual *Finance and General Rating Statistics*, Chartered Institute of Public Finance and Accountancy. Summary tables on taxes, rates, etc., are published yearly in the *Annual Abstract of Statistics*, HMSO.

Chapter 4

A convenient analysis of government borrowing and its uses is in the Treasury's *Economic Progress Report*, No. 136, August 1981. Regular official reports of activities in the money markets appear in the *Bank of England Quarterly Bulletin*, and events are most fully discussed and reported in *The Financial Times*. For discussion of the lack of parliamentary control, see the *House of Commons Procedure (Supply) Committee 1st Re-*

port, HC 118 (1980–81). For details of the system of local authority borrowing, see Labour Party, *Local Government Handbook*, The Labour Party 1981. For an account of how the City see local councils as a safe place to invest, see Phillips and Drew, *Local Authorities in Britain*, Phillips & Drew 1977.

For the influence of the money markets generally, and specific discussion of the 1975–77 pressures, see W. Keegan and R. Pennant-Rea, *Who Runs the Economy?*, Maurice Temple Smith 1979.

The basic source on the real cost of the national debt is an article in *Economic Trends*, May 1977. Regular updates of the data are given in *Financial Statistics*, and articles in the *Bank of England Quarterly Bulletin* also cover the issue.

Chapter 5

The outstanding account of the planning process is H. Heclo and A. Wildavsky, *The Private Government of Public Money* (second edition), Macmillan 1981, which gives a highly readable account of how the system works. A brief account is also given in CSE State Group, *Struggle over the State*, CSE Books 1979, in the chapter on fiscal control. A critical analysis by public service unions was published as *Behind Closed Doors*, National Steering Committee Against the Cuts 1979. Some of the themes of this have since been echoed in TUC *Economic Reviews*, e.g. 1981 and 1982. Critical accounts of the cash limits system are thin on the ground. Official accounts, like the original White Paper *Cash Limits*, HMSO 1976, Cmnd.6440, tend to obscure the most important points. Accounts of their effects are increasing in number: see for instance H. Glennerster in D. Hood and M. Wright (eds.), *Big Government, Hard Times*, Martin Robertson 1981, on the effect on social services, or R. Hill, in *Socialist Economic Review 1983*, Merlin Press (forthcoming, 1983), on the effects on housing.

On the parliamentary role see Ann Robinson, *Parliament and Public Spending*, Heinemann 1978, for a liberal critique of the limitations on parliament. A useful factual review of the constitutional position is contained in the *House of Commons*

Procedure (Supply) Committee 1st Report, HC 118 (1980–81).

Chapter 6

A readable and reliable history of the role of the district auditor is contained in the *Haldane Bulletin*, Nos. 14 and 15, 1981. A briefer account appeared in *Labour Research*, February 1982.

For details of the main sources on local government finance and controls, see notes to Chapter 2. The latest systems of central control are described in two articles in *Labour Research*, March 1982 and October 1982. An overview of all the various controls and pressures is in a feature in *Community Action*, No. 56, 1982.

On other services, NHS politics and finance are discussed in Lesley Doyal with Imogen Pennell, *The Political Economy of Health*, Pluto Press 1979; the system of housing finance is described by H. Aughton, *Housing Finance*, Shelter 1982.

Chapter 7

There is a sad lack of detailed studies of working conditions of public employees. The best sources are union journals and pamphlets. Virtually no governmental, parliamentary or academic literature on the economics of public spending or the machinery of public administration spend any time at all on workers' experiences.

Among the few academic discussions of union organisation in the public services are Pete Fairbrother, *Working for the State*, Workers' Education Association 1982; and Bob Fryer, 'British Trade Unions and the Cuts', *Capital and Class*, No. 8, 1979. A book which covers the experience of managerialism in local councils is Cynthia Cockburn, *The Local State*, Pluto Press 1977.

Responses to privatisation have produced some useful literature. An excellent example is an education pack published by the London Region of the National Union of Public Employees.

Chapter 8

The standard formulations of the 'Alternative Economic Strategy' are in the CSE London Group, *The Alternative Economic Strategy*, CSE Books 1980; and in Sam Aaronovitch, *The Road from Thatcherism*, Lawrence & Wishart 1981.

The versions developed by the Labour movement establishment are in the TUC's *Economic Reviews* 1981 and 1982, and the TUC/Labour Party document *Economic Planning and Industrial Democracy*, 1982.

Critiques of the AES have come from various parts of the left, and on various grounds (e.g. it won't work, it won't be helpful if it does work, it won't help women, it won't help workers, it will only help profitability, it would be steamrollered out of sight by capital anyway). Easy sources for some of the main lines of criticism are Andrew Glyn and John Harrison, *The British Economic Disaster*, Pluto Press 1980; and the *Socialist Economic Review 1982*, Merlin Press 1982.

Chapter 9

The quotations in the final section come from *Direct Building*, Labour Research Department 1929; and Karl Marx, 'Instructions for Delegates to the Geneva Congress' (1866), in *The First International and After*, Penguin 1974.